ROCKFORD CORPORATION:
AN ACCOUNTING PRACTICE SET

DONALD E. KIESO, Ph.D., C.P.A.

KPMG Emeritus Professor of Accountancy
Northern Illinois University
DeKalb, Illinois

JERRY J. WEYGANDT, Ph.D., C.P.A.

Arthur Andersen Alumni Emeritus Professor of Accounting
University of Wisconsin
Madison, Wisconsin

TERRY D. WARFIELD, Ph.D.

PricewaterhouseCoopers Research Scholar
University of Wisconsin
Madison, Wisconsin

PREPARED BY
LARRY FALCETTO, C.P.A., C.M.A.

Associate Professor of Accounting
Emporia State University
Emporia, Kansas

John Wiley & Sons, Inc.

COVER PHOTO ©James Rudnick/The Stock Market.

To order books or for customer service call 1-800-CALL-WILEY (225-5945).

ISBN-13 978-0-470-38063-5

Printed in the United States of America

10 9 8 7 6 5 4 3 2 1

Printed and bound by Bind-Rite, Inc.

PREFACE

This accounting practice set has been prepared for use in conjunction with Chapter 3, "The Accounting Information System," from *Intermediate Accounting*, by Donald E. Kieso, Jerry J. Weygandt, and Terry D. Warfield. It has been designed as a student's review and update of the accounting cycle and the preparation of financial statements that are covered in the traditional first-year principles of financial accounting course. It is a review of elementary accounting and an application of the contents of Chapter 3 of *Intermediate Accounting*; it should be used at the beginning of intermediate accounting, not at the end.

Two versions of this practice set are provided. The first version uses the periodic inventory method; the second version of the practice set, starting on page 77, uses the perpetual inventory method.

Completion of this practice set requires (1) analyzing transactions, (2) journalizing transactions, (3) posting to the general ledger and two subsidiary ledgers, (4) preparing year-end adjusting entries, (5) using a ten-column work sheet, (6) preparing financial statements, and (7) closing the accounts. The required portion of this practice set should take between 11 to 14 hours to work. The optional assignment (number 12, preparation of a statement of cash flows) takes an additional 1 to $1\frac{1}{2}$ hours to work.

An alternative set of instructions is contained on pages 17-19 and is to be worked only if assigned by the instructor in place of the instructions on pages 14-16. The alternative set is not different in level of difficulty or time needed to complete the work. Only the adjusting entries, account balances, and financial statement contents are different.

CONTENTS

ROCKFORD CORPORATION

A PRACTICE SET TO ACCOMPANY

Intermediate Accounting, by Kieso, Weygandt, and Warfield

PERIODIC INVENTORY

Narrative and Instructions

Rockford Corporation is a wholesale plumbing supply distributor. The corporation was organized in 1981, under the laws of the State of Illinois, with an authorized capitalization of 10,000 shares of no-par common stock with a stated value of $30 per share. The common stock is sold over the counter in the local area. You have been hired as of Monday, December 27, 2010, to replace the controller, who has resigned. As controller, you are responsible for the corporation's accounting records, preparation of the financial statements, safeguarding the corporate assets, and providing management with financial information to set prices and to monitor and control operations. You have an assistant who keeps the payroll records, the plant asset ledger, and the perpetual inventory (by quantity only). The corporation secretary maintains the stockholder records, and the receptionist/secretary acts as the petty cashier.

Rockford Corporation closes its books annually on December 31 but prepares financial statements quarterly. Adjusting entries are posted to the general ledger only at year-end; at the end of the first, second, and third quarter the adjustments are entered only on a ten-column work sheet, not in the general ledger. Therefore, *the adjusting entries to be recorded on December 31 are annual adjustments* that you must journalize and then post to the general ledger accounts before preparing the financial statements.

Rockford Corporation maintains a quantity-only perpetual inventory system and takes a physical count on December 31 to cost the inventory on hand and to adjust the inventory carrying amount per the general ledger. Purchases are recorded at the gross amount (discounts taken are recognized at the date of payment) of the supplier's invoice, and the terms vary with each supplier. Sales on account are subject to terms of 2/10, n/30. Discounts are taken and granted only when the terms are met. The corporation uses the following journals and ledgers:

JOURNALS

1. A sales journal (S)–to record sales of merchandise on account.
2. A purchases journal (P)–to record purchases of merchandise on account.
3. A cash receipts journal (CR)–to record all cash receipts.
4. A cash disbursements journal (CD)–to record all cash payments.
5. A general journal (J)–to record all transactions that cannot be recorded in the other journals.

LEDGERS

1. A general ledger.
2. An accounts receivable subsidiary ledger.
3. An accounts payable subsidiary ledger.

In recording sales transactions, each sale should be posted on the day of the sale directly to the customer's account in the subsidiary ledger, using the invoice number as the posting reference number in the subsidiary account. Also, cash receipts from customers should be posted to the subsidiary ledger on the day they are received. The purchase order number should be used as the posting reference number in the subsidiary ledger for purchases on account from suppliers. Purchases from suppliers and payments to them should be posted daily. All other individual posting may be made weekly or at the month-end. Account numbers should be used as posting reference numbers in the journals.

Officers, sales, and office personnel are salaried employees and are paid monthly on the last day of each month. The delivery truck drivers and warehouse employees are hourly wage employees and are paid biweekly. Each biweekly pay period ends Friday. On the following Monday your assistant, who maintains the payroll records, provides you with a payroll summary from which you prepare general journal entries to record the biweekly payroll and the employer's taxes on the payroll. The biweekly employees' paychecks are distributed on the following day (Tuesday).

The general ledger chart of accounts is shown below:

CHART OF ACCOUNTS

Accounts	Account Number
Cash	101
Petty Cash	105
Accounts Receivable	112
Allowance for Doubtful Accounts	113
Notes Receivable	115
Interest Receivable	118
Merchandise Inventory	120
Office Supplies	125
Prepaid Insurance	130
Prepaid Rent	131
Other Assets	135
Land	140
Buildings	145
Accum. Depr.–Buildings	146
Office Equipment	151
Accum. Depr.–Off. Equip.	152
Delivery Trucks	163
Accum. Depr.–Delivery Trucks	164
Notes Payable	200
Accounts Payable	201
Wages Payable	211
Salaries Payable	212
FICA Taxes Payable	214
Federal Income Taxes Payable	215
Federal Income Tax Withholding Payable	216
State Income Tax Withholding Payable	218
Federal Unemployment Taxes Payable	224
State Unemployment Taxes Payable	226
Interest Payable	230
Dividends Payable	250
Notes Payable (LT Liability)	268
Bonds Payable	270
Discount on Bonds Payable	273
Common Stock	311
P-I-C in Excess of Stated Value	317
Retained Earnings	320
Treasury Stock-Common	330
Dividends Declared	333
Income Summary	350
Sales	401
Sales Returns and Allowances	412
Sales Discounts	414
Purchases	510
Purchases Returns and Allowances	512
Purchases Discounts	514
Freight-in	516
Advertising Expenses	610
Bad Debt Expense	612
Depreciation Expense-Trucks	617
Sales Salaries Expense	627
Wage Expense	643
Freight-out	644
Miscellaneous Selling Expense	649
Depreciation Expense–Buildings	713
Depreciation Expense–Off. Equip.	715
Insurance Expense	722
Office Salaries Expense	727
Office Supplies Expense	728
Rent Expenses	729
Payroll Taxes Expense	730
Utilities Expense	732
Interest Revenue	820
Gain on Plant Assets	826
Interest Expense	905
Loss on Plant Assets	921
Income Tax Expense	999

The January 1, 2010, balances appear in the general ledger accounts as well as the November 30, 2010, balances, for those accounts whose balances have changed. All transactions affecting the non-current accounts from January 1, 2010, through November 30, 2010, with explanations, appear in these accounts to facilitate the preparation of the statement of cash flows.

Subsidiary ledger account balances as of November 30, 2010, are as follows (the balances appear in the appropriate subsidiary ledger accounts):

ACCOUNTS RECEIVABLE

Boecker Builders	$62,920
The Potts Company	50,300
Swanson Brothers Construction	24,050
Trudy's Plumbing	15,100
Coconino Contractors, Inc.	27,800
Rankin Plumbing Corp.	74,350
Beverly's Building Products	14,000
Bilder Construction Company	45,200
Iwanaga Plumbing and Heating	3,700
Total accounts receivable	$317,420

ACCOUNTS PAYABLE

Phoenix Plastics	$17,450
Edward's Plumbing Supplies, Inc.	20,050
Oxenford Copperworks	26,400
Smith Pipe Company	38,100
Ron & Rod's Plumbing Products	14,850
Khatan Steel Corp.	10,000
Total accounts payable	$126,850

The transactions through December 23 have already been recorded by the former controller. You are to begin your work by entering the transaction of December 27 for the payment of cash to repurchase stock.

DECEMBER 2010

S	M	T	W	T	F	S
			1	2	3	4
5	6	7	8	9	10	11
12	13	14	15	16	17	18
19	20	21	22	23	24	25
26	27	28	29	30	31	

NARRATIVE OF THE DECEMBER TRANSACTIONS

NOTE: All transactions from Dec. 1 thru Dec. 23
have already been recorded

December

1   Received a check in the amount of $23,569 from Swanson Brothers Construction in full payment of invoice No. 1120 dated November 26 in the amount of $24,050.

1   Sold sewer and drainage pipe to Beverly's Building Products on account, invoice No. 1201 for $13,150.

2   Purchased copper tubing and fittings from Edward's Plumbing Supplies Inc. on account, purchase order No. 315 for $24,320, terms n/60.

2   Issued check No. 1580 for $26,400 to Oxenford Copperworks in settlement of the balance owed on purchase order No. 280.

3   A court notice indicates that Iwanaga Plumbing and Heating is bankrupt and payment of its account improbable; the president orders the account to be written off as a bad debt (invoice No. 780).

3   Sold bathroom fixtures to Bilder Construction Company on account, invoice No.1202 for $44,900.

6   Received a check in the amount of $49,294 from The Potts Company in full payment of invoice No. 1128 dated November 27 for $50,300.

6   Sold plumbing supplies and plastic pipe to Coconino Contractors, Inc. on account, invoice No. 1203 for $10,300.

6   Issued check No. 1581 for $810 to Standard Oil Co. in payment of gas, oil, and truck repair from Tierney's Standard Service.

7   Issued check No. 1582 for $9,900 to Khatan Steel Corp. in full settlement of purchase order No. 312 for $10,000.

7   Issued check No. 1583 for $10,486 to Phoenix Plastics in full payment of Phoenix's invoice dated November 28 in the amount of $10,700, for purchase order No. 313, terms 2/10, n/30.

7   Received a check in the amount of $72,863 from Rankin Plumbing Corp. in full payment of invoice No. 1129 dated November 28 for $74,350.

7   The payroll summary for the biweekly pay period ended Friday, December 3 contained the following information:

Delivery and warehouse wages	$4,860
FICA taxes withheld	350
Federal income taxes withheld	900
State income taxes withheld	190
Net pay	$3,420
Employer's payroll taxes:	
FICA tax	$ 350
Federal unemployment tax	–
State unemployment tax	–

Issued check No. 1584 for the amount of the net pay and deposited it in the payroll bank account. Individual payroll checks were then prepared for distribution to the biweekly employees on Tuesday, December 7.

8 Sold cast pipe to Trudy's Plumbing on account, invoice No. 1204 for $26,300.

8 Received a check in the amount of $27,800 from Coconino Contractors, Inc. in full payment of invoice No. 1091 dated October 20.

8 Purchased bathroom fixtures from Phoenix Plastics, on account, purchase order No. 316 for $52,700 terms 1/10, n/30.

9 Received a check in the amount of $29,000 from Boecker Builders in partial payment of balance outstanding covering invoice Nos. 1050 and 1071.

9 Issued check No. 1585 for $600 to Scooter Gordon for lettering and sign painting on some delivery trucks.

9 Issued check No. 1586 for $6,750 to Phoenix Plastics, in payment of Phoenix's invoice dated November 10 in the amount of $6,750, our purchase order No. 299.

10 Issued check No. 1587 for $37,719 to Smith Pipe Company in full payment of their invoice dated November 28, terms 1/15, n/60, our purchase order No. 314.

10 Received a check in the amount of $15,100 from Trudy's Plumbing in full settlement of invoice No. 1106 dated November 7.

10 Sold pipe, fixtures, and accessories to Trudy's Plumbing on account, invoice No. 1205 for $24,850.

13 Sold plumbing supplies and copper tubing to The Potts Company on account, invoice No. 1206 for $31,450

13 Received a check in the amount of $33,920 from Boecker Builders in full payment of invoice No. 1071.

13 Cash sales to date totaled $12,292.

14 Received a check in the amount of $25,774 from Trudy's Plumbing in payment of invoice No. 1204.

14 Sold plumbing fixtures and supplies to Boecker Builders, on account, invoice No. 1207 for $21,730.

15 The Potts Company returned defective copper tubing that it purchased on December 10. A credit memo in the amount of $4,680 is issued relative to invoice No. 1206.

15 The defective copper tubing is returned to Edward's Plumbing Supplies, Inc. along with a debit memo in the amount of $3,550 in reduction of purchase order No. 315.

15 Issued check No. 1588 for $399 in payment of November telephone bill to Northern Illinois Communications.

16 Issued check No. 1589 in the amount of $11,360 in payment of federal withholding taxes, $9,573, and FICA taxes, $1,787, payable on November salaries and wages; the check is remitted to the Winnebago County Bank as the depository.

16 Issued check No. 1590 for $52,173 to Phoenix Plastics, Inc. in payment of purchase order No. 316.

17 The president informs you that Bilder Construction Company agrees to convert the $45,200 overdue account receivable (invoice No. 1120) to a 14% note due six months from today.

17 Purchased plumbing materials from Smith Pipe Company on account, purchase order No. 317 for $43,800 terms 1/15, n/60.

17 Sold drain tile, plastic pipe, and copper tubing to A & B Hardware on account, invoice No. 1208 for $7,920.

20 Sold fixtures and materials to Coconino Contractors, Inc. on account, invoice No. 1209 for $42,780.

20 An invoice in the amount of $1,021 was received from S. White Trucking Company for transportation-in on purchase order No. 317 and paid by issuing check No. 1591.

20 Received a check in the amount of $24,353 from Trudy's Plumbing in payment of invoice No. 1205.

21 Purchased office supplies from the Pen & Pad, issuing check No. 1592 in the amount of $1,360. (Note: Debit asset account).

21 The payroll summary for the biweekly pay period ended Friday, December 17, contained the following information:

Delivery and warehouse wages	$5,770
FICA taxes withheld	415
Federal income taxes withheld	1,067
State income taxes withheld	225
Net pay	$4,063

Employer's payroll taxes:	
FICA tax	$ 415
Federal unemployment tax	–
State unemployment tax	–

Issued check No. 1593 for the amount of the net pay and deposited it in the payroll bank account. Individual payroll checks were then prepared for distribution to the biweekly employees on Tuesday, December 21.

22 Purchased a new Faith computer for $6,100 from Business Basics, Inc., purchase order No. 318, paying $600 down through Check No. 1594 with the balance due in thirty days (n/30). The computer has an estimated life of five years with a salvage value of $1,300. Use subsidiary account No. 16. Journalize the entire entry in the cash disbursements journal.

22 Purchased bathroom and kitchen fixtures from Phoenix Plastics, on account, purchase order No. 319 for $48,330, terms 1/10, n/30.

23 Received a bill from DeKalb Transport for $2,300 for transportation-in costs incurred during the last 30 days, terms n/30.

NOTE: Transactions up to this point have been recorded. At this point you became controller and are responsible for recording all further transactions.

27 The board of directors voted to purchase 1,000 shares of its own stock from stockholder Dionne Schivone at $83 per share and issued check No. 1595 in payment. Stock repurchases are recorded at cost. Rockford is purchasing these shares because Ms. Schivone had been a valuable employee.

27 The board of directors declared a $2.70 per-share cash dividend payable on January 14 to stockholders of record on December 27 (after purchase of stock).

27 The president informs you that Beverly's Building Products agrees to convert the $14,000 overdue accounts receivable (invoice No. 1119) balance to a 12% note due six months from today.

28 A half-acre parcel of land adjacent to the building is acquired in exchange for 600 shares of unissued common stock. The land has a fair value of $54,000 and will be used immediately as an outside storage lot and parking lot.

28 An invoice in the amount of $2,650 is received from Wayne McManus, lawyer, for legal services involved in the acquisition of the adjacent parcel of land; check No. 1596 is issued in payment.

28 Sold pipe and plumbing materials to Boecker Builders on account, invoice No. 1210 for $42,040.

29 Issued check No. 1597 in the amount of $500 to the *Northern Star* for advertisement run in the home building supplement of December 15.

29 Issued check No. 1598 in the amount of $925 to Standard Oil Co. in payment of gas, oil, and truck repairs from Standard Oil Co. (use Freight-out).

29 Purchased copper and cast iron pipe from Oxenford Copperworks on account, purchase order No. 320 for $55,940, terms 1/10, n/30.

29 Check No. 1599 for $15,000 is issued to the bond sinking fund trustee, Chicago Trust Co., for deposit in the sinking fund (use Other Assets).

30 Received a check for $21,730 from Boecker Builders in payment of invoice No. 1207.

30 Sold plumbing supplies to Swanson Brothers Construction on account, invoice No. 1211 for $24,650.

30 Issued check No. 1600 for $43,362 to Smith Pipe Company in payment of purchase order No. 317.

31 The custodian of the petty cash fund submits the following receipts for reimbursement and reports a cash-on-hand count of $8.

Postage stamps used	$38
United Parcel (freight-out)	23
C.O.D. postage (freight-in)	51
Christmas office decorations	30

Check No. 1601 is issued and cashed to reimburse the fund.

31 Sold an electric truck-lift to Leila Stierman Co. for $2,500 cash. The original cost was $7,900 with salvage value of $900, a life of 10 years, and accumulated depreciation recorded through 12/31/09 of $4,550. The straight-line method is used. (Note: the company follows the practice of recording a half year's depreciation in the year of acquisition and a half year in the year of disposal.) First, bring the depreciation expense up to date in the general journal. Then journalize the entire entry for the sale in the cash receipts journal.

31 Sold bathroom fixtures and plumbing supplies to Trudy's Plumbing on account, invoice No. 1212 for $55,770.

31 Because for some time the petty cash fund has been smaller than required for monthly expenditures, the fund is increased by $75 by cashing check No. 1602 and placing the money in the petty cash fund.

31 The payroll summary for the *monthly* paid employees is submitted so that December checks can be distributed before the year-end; the details are as follows:

Sales salaries...	$16,000
Office and administrative salaries............................	22,900
Federal income taxes withheld	7,196
State income taxes withheld	1,517
FICA taxes withheld	2,120
Net pay..	$28,067

Issued check No. 1603 for the amount of the net pay and deposited it in the payroll bank account. Individual payroll checks were prepared for distribution to all monthly employees by the end of the day.

Employer's payroll taxes:	
FICA tax (all office and administrative)..........	$2,120
Federal unemployment tax..............................	–
State unemployment tax	–

31   Cash sales since December 13 total $25,980.

INSTRUCTIONS

1. Make the entries in the appropriate journals for December 27 through December 31.

2. Post any amounts to be posted as individual amounts from the journals to the general ledger and any amounts to be posted to the subsidiary ledger accounts. (If the normal practice of daily posting were followed, the postings would be in chronological order; proper date sequence for this practice set is not necessary.)

3. Foot and cross-foot the columnar journals and complete the month-end postings of all books of original entry.

4. Prepare a trial balance by entering the account balances from the general ledger in the first two columns of the ten-column work sheet (list all accounts, including those with zero balances).

5. From the following information prepare adjusting entries in the general journal and enter them in the "adjustments" columns of the work sheet and cross-reference the amounts using the related alphabetic characters (round all calculations to the nearest dollar).

   a. The annual provision for doubtful accounts receivable is recorded by providing a charge to Bad Debt Expense in an amount equal to 2% of net sales. (This entry should be entered below the middle of General Journal page 10.)

   b. An inventory count of the office supplies revealed $830 of supplies on hand at year-end.

   c. A physical inventory on Friday, January 7, 2011, results in a total dollar value assigned to the ending inventory at lower of cost or market of $539,930 (use Income Summary account for adjustment purposes).

d. The insurance premium outstanding on January 1, 2010, covers the period January 1 through August 31, 2010. The insurance premium of $7,050 recorded in August covers the period of September 1, 2010 through August 31, 2011. Rockford estimates that 75% of the premiums are attributable to general activities and 25% to selling activities (use Miscellaneous Selling Expense).

e. The payroll summary for the employees who are paid biweekly shows the following information at December 31, 2010:

Delivery and Warehouse Wages	$5,600
FICA Taxes Payable	375
Federal Withholding Taxes	1,036
State Withholding Taxes...	218
Net pay..	$3,971

f. The employer's share of the FICA tax ($375) must be accrued; no state or federal unemployment tax is incurred during the fourth quarter because all wages and salaries earned during the last quarter exceed the maximum subject to unemployment tax.

g. Interest has accrued at 8% on the mortgage notes payable since July 1, 2010. The next six-month interest payment at 9% on the bonds is due on March 1, 2011. The discount on bonds payable has not been amortized for any part of 2010; the bonds are dated March 1, 2004, and mature March 1, 2014. (Use straight-line.)

h. The interest accrued to 12/31/10 on notes receivable is composed of the following:

Platteville Plumbers, 10%, 6 months, due March 31, 2011	$1,125
Bilder Construction, 11%, 6 months, due June 14, 2011	232
Beverly's Building, 9%, 6 months, due June 26, 2011	17
	$1,374

The interest accrued at 12/31/10 on the note payable of $15,000 @ 10% is $1,500. Interest is payable on January 2, 2011. (The note is due in 2011.)

i. A warehouse lease payment of $10,890 was made on September 1, 2010, for rental through February 28, 2011. (The Prepaid Rent account is for advance lease payments on the warehouse.)

j. $530 is owed to Northern Electric Co. and $279 is owed to City of Rockford for utility services provided during December 2010.

k. Plant and equipment to be depreciated are composed of the following:

Assets	Date Acquired	Cost	Estimated Usage or Life	Salvage Value	Depreciation Method
Building	7/1/06	$306,000	25 years	$20,000	sum-of-the-years' digits
Truck No. 1	4/1/07	28,000	60,000 miles	3,100	miles driven
Truck No. 2	9/1/09	33,000	60,000 miles	4,200	miles driven
Lift No. 1 (Sold 12/31/10)	8/17/03	7,900	10 years	900	straight-line
Lift No. 2	3/29/07	4,500	10 years	500	straight-line
Lift No. 3	9/16/08	5,000	10 years	500	straight-line
Office Equipment	All prior to 1/1/10	32,800	7 years	2,000	straight-line
Computer	12/22/10	6,100	5 years	1,300	Double-decling balance

Truck No. 1 has been driven 45,000 miles prior to 1/1/10 and truck No. 2 has been driven 30,500 miles prior to 1/1/10. During 2010 truck No. 1 was driven 12,000 miles and truck No. 2 was driven 14,000 miles. Remember that the Rockford Company takes a half-year's depreciation in the year of acquisition and a half-year in the year of sale.

6. Complete the work sheet. In completing the worksheet, compute State of Illinois corporate income taxes at 4½% of pretax income. The state income tax is deductible on the federal tax return, and the federal tax is *not* deductible on the Illinois return. Assume federal corporate income tax on income subject to federal tax is as follows:

   first $50,000   @15%
   next 25,000   @25%
   remainder   @34%

   Income between $100,000 and $335,000 is assessed a 5% federal surtax, not to exceed $11,750.

   Hint: Corporations subject to federal income tax must make estimated tax payments throughout the year. At the time of the payment, the account Income Tax Expense is debited and Cash is credited. To determine the taxable income at year end, net the total debits and total credits from the income statement in the worksheet. Note that the estimated income tax expense is listed as a debit and must be subtracted from total debits when determining taxable income (federal tax is not a deductible item).

7. Prepare the journal entry for income taxes. Post all adjusting entries.

8. Prepare schedules of subsidiary accounts receivable and accounts payable and determine that the total per each subsidiary schedule agrees with the related control account.

9. Prepare an income statement (assume the weighted-average number of shares outstanding for the year 2010 is 5,600 shares). Assume that bad debt expense is an administrative expense. Assume that payroll taxes expense is 80% administrative.

10. Prepare a statement of retained earnings.

11. Prepare a balance sheet. (Hint: combine Petty Cash with Cash for balance sheet purposes.)

12. *OPTIONAL ASSIGNMENT* (1 to 1½ hours): Prepare a statement of cash flows using the indirect approach. (Hint: combine Petty Cash with Cash for purposes of determining changes in cash.)

13. Prepare and post closing entries.

14. Prepare a post-closing trial balance.

AN ALTERNATIVE SET OF INSTRUCTIONS
FOR ROCKFORD CORPORATION

To the Student: These pages contain a second set of instructions which, if assigned by the instructor, are to be utilized in place of pages 14-16. The primary differences between these two sets are in the adjusting entries, instruction steps 5 through 9. All other information, forms, and requirements are the same.

ALTERNATIVE SET OF INSTRUCTIONS

1. Make the entries in the appropriate journals for December 27 through December 31.

2. Post any amounts to be posted as individual amounts from the journals to the general ledger and any amounts to be posted to the subsidiary ledger accounts. (If the normal practice of daily posting were followed, the postings would be in chronological order; proper date sequence for this practice set is not necessary.)

3. Foot and cross-foot the columnar journals and complete the month-end postings of all books of original entry.

4. Prepare a trial balance by entering the account balances from the general ledger in the first two columns of the ten-column work sheet (list all accounts, including those with zero balances).

5. From the following information prepare adjusting entries in the general journal and enter them in the "adjustments" columns of the work sheet and cross-reference the amounts using the related alphabetic characters (round all calculations to the nearest dollar).

    a. The annual provision for doubtful accounts receivable is recorded by providing a charge to Bad Debt Expense in an amount equal to 1½% of net sales. (This entry should be entered below the middle of General Journal page 10.)

    b. An inventory count of the office supplies revealed $810 of supplies on hand at year-end.

    c. A physical inventory on Wednesday, January 2, 2011, results in a total dollar value assigned to the ending inventory at lower of cost or market of $543,200 (use Income Summary account for adjustment purposes).

    d. The insurance premium outstanding on January 1, 2010, covers the period January 1 through August 31, 2010. The insurance premium of $7,050 recorded in August covers the period of September 1, 2010 through August 31, 2011. Rockford estimates that 80% of the premiums are attributable to general activities and 20% to selling activities (use Miscellaneous Selling Expense).

e. The payroll summary for the employees who are paid biweekly shows the following information at December 31, 2010:

Delivery and Warehouse Wages	$5,300
FICA Taxes Payable	360
Federal Withholding Taxes	980
State Withholding Taxes...	200
Net pay..	$3,760

f. The employer's share of the FICA tax ($360) must be accrued; no state or federal unemployment tax is incurred during the fourth quarter because all wages and salaries earned during the last quarter exceed the maximum subject to unemployment tax.

g. Interest has accrued at 9% on the long-term notes payable since July 1, 2010. The next six-month interest payment at 9% on the bonds is due on March 1, 2011. The discount on bonds payable has not been amortized for any part of 2010; the bonds are dated March 1, 2004, and mature March 1, 2014.

h. The interest accrued to 12/31/10 on notes receivable is composed of the following:

Platteville Plumbers, 11%, 6 months, due March 31, 2011	$1,237
Bilder Construction, 10%, 6 months, due June 14, 2011	211
Beverly's Building, 9%, 6 months, due June 26, 2011	17
	$1,465

The interest accrued at 12/31/10 on the note payable of $15,000 @ 10% is $1,500. Interest is payable on January 2, 2011.

i. A warehouse lease payment of $10,890 was made on September 1, 2010, for rental through February 28, 2011. (The Prepaid Rent account is for advance lease payments on the warehouse.)

j. $590 is owed to Northern Electric Co. and $270 is owed to City of Rockford for utility services provided during December 2010.

k. Plant and equipment to be depreciated are composed of the following:

Assets	Date Acquired	Cost	Estimated Usage or Life	Salvage Value	Depreciation Method
Building	7/1/06	$306,000	25 years	$20,000	sum-of-the-years' digits
Truck No. 1	4/1/07	28,000	60,000 miles	3,100	miles driven
Truck No. 2	9/1/09	33,000	60,000 miles	4,200	miles driven
Lift No. 1 (Sold 12/31/10)	8/17/03	7,900	10 years	900	straight-line
Lift No. 2	3/29/07	4,500	10 years	500	straight-line
Lift No. 3	9/16/08	5,000	10 years	500	straight-line
Office Equipment	All prior to 1/1/10	32,800	7 years	2,000	straight-line
Computer	12/22/10	6,100	6 years	1,300	Double-decling balance

Truck No. 1 has been driven 45,000 miles prior to 1/1/10 and truck No. 2 has been driven 30,500 miles prior to 1/1/10. During 2010 truck No. 1 was driven 15,000 miles and truck No. 2 was driven 12,000 miles. Remember that the Rockford Company takes a half-year's depreciation in the year of acquisition and a half-year in the year of sale.

6. Complete the work sheet. In completing the worksheet, compute State of Illinois corporate income taxes at 4% of pretax income. The state income tax is deductible on the federal tax return, and the federal tax is *not* deductible on the Illinois return. Assume federal corporate income tax on income subject to federal tax is as follows:

first $50,000	@15%
next 25,000	@25%
remainder	@34%

Income between $100,000 and $335,000 is assessed a 5% federal surtax, not to exceed $11,750.

Hint: Corporations subject to federal income tax must make estimated tax payments throughout the year. At the time of the payment, the account Income Tax Expense is debited and Cash is credited. To determine the taxable income at year end, net the total debits and total credits from the income statement in the worksheet. Note that the estimated income tax expense is listed as a debit and must be subtracted from total debits when determining taxable income (federal tax is not a deductible item).

7. Prepare the journal entry for income taxes. Post all adjusting entries.

8. Prepare schedules of subsidiary accounts receivable and accounts payable and determine that the total per each subsidiary schedule agrees with the related control account.

9. Prepare an income statement (assume the weighted-average number of shares outstanding for the year 2010 is 5,592 shares). Assume that bad debt expense is an administrative expense. Assume payroll taxes expense is 80% administrative.

10. Prepare a statement of retained earnings.

11. Prepare a balance sheet. (Hint: combine Petty Cash with Cash for balance sheet purposes.)

12. *OPTIONAL ASSIGNMENT* (1 to 1½ hours): Prepare a statement of cash flows using the indirect approach. (Hint: combine Petty Cash with Cash for purposes of determining changes in cash.)

13. Prepare and post closing entries.

14. Prepare a post-closing trial balance.

JOURNALS

GENERAL JOURNAL
PURCHASES JOURNAL
SALES JOURNAL
CASH RECEIPTS JOURNAL
CASH DISBURSEMENTS JOURNAL

GENERAL JOURNAL — Page 9

DATE 2010		Account Titles and Explanation	REF.	DEBIT	CREDIT
12	3	Allowance for Doubtful Accounts	113	3700	
		Accounts Receivable–Iwanaga Plumbing and Heating	112/190		3700
		To record the write-off of an			
		account due to bankruptcy.			
12	7	Payroll Taxes Expense	730	350	
		FICA Taxes Payable	214		350
		To record employer's portion of			
		FICA taxes on biweekly payroll.			
12	15	Sales Returns and Allowances	412	4680	
		Accounts Receivable–The Potts Company	112/122		4680
		To record defective copper tubing returned			
		by customer.			
12	15	Accounts Payable–Edward's Plumbing Supplies, Inc.	201/18	3550	
		Purchases Returns and Allowances	512		3550
		To record defective copper tubing returned			
		to supplier.			
12	17	Notes Receivable	115	45200	
		Accounts Receivable–Bilder Construction	112/180		45200
		To record receipt of a 14%, 6-month			
		note for an overdue accounts receivable			
12	21	Payroll Taxes Expense	730	415	
		FICA Taxes Payable	214		415
		To record employer's portion of			
		FICA taxes on biweekly payroll			
12	23	Freight-In	516	2300	
		Accounts Payable–DeKalb Transport	201/20		2300
		To record freight costs for December, 2010			

DATE 2010		Account Titles and Explanation	REF.	DEBIT	CREDIT
ADJUSTING ENTRIES AT 12/31/10					

DATE 2010	Account Titles and Explanation	REF.	DEBIT	CREDIT

DATE 2010		Account Titles and Explanation	REF.	DEBIT	CREDIT

DATE 2010		Account Titles and Explanation	REF.	DEBIT	CREDIT
		CLOSING ENTRIES AT 12/31/10			

DATE 2010		Account Titles and Explanation	REF.	DEBIT	CREDIT

DATE 2010		PUR. ORDER NO.	ACCOUNT CREDITED	ACCT. NO.	AMOUNT	
12	2	315	Edward's Plumbing Supplies, Inc. n/60	18	24	320
	8	316	Phoenix Plastics 1/10, n/30	14	52	700
	17	317	Smith Pipe Company 1/15, n/60	39	43	800
	22	318	(see Cash Disbursements Journal)			
	22	319	Phoenix Plastics 1/10, n/30	14	48	330

DATE 2010		INVOICE NO.	ACCOUNT DEBITED	ACCT. NO.	AMOUNT	
12	1	1201	Beverly's Building Products	175	13	150
	3	1202	Bilder Construction Co.	180	44	900
	6	1203	Coconino Contractors, Inc.	160	10	300
	8	1204	Trudy's Plumbing	155	26	300
	10	1205	Trudy's Plumbing	155	24	850
	13	1206	The Potts Company	122	31	450
	14	1207	Boecker Builders	117	21	730
	17	1208	A & B Hardware	143	7	920
	20	1209	Coconino Contractors, Inc.	160	42	780

DATE 2010		DESCRIPTION	CASH DR	SALES DISCOUNTS DR	REF	ACCOUNTS RECEIVABLE CR	SALES CR	SUNDRY ACCOUNTS			
								ACCT NO.	✓	DR	CR
12	1	Swanson Brothers Construction	23569	481	133	24050					
	6	The Potts Company	49294	1006	122	50300					
	7	Rankin Plumbing Corp.	72863	1487	166	74350					
	8	Coconino Contractors, Inc.	27800		160	27800					
	9	Boecker Builders	29000		117	29000					
	10	Trudy's Plumbing	15100		155	15100					
	13	Boecker Builders	33920		117	33920					
	13	Cash sales	12292				12292				
	14	Trudy's Plumbing	25774	526	155	26300					
	20	Trudy's Plumbing	24353	497	155	24850					

DATE 2010		CHECK NO.	PAYEE	CASH CR	REF	ACCOUNTS PAYABLE DR	PUR. DISC. CR	SUNDRY ACCOUNTS			
								ACCT NO.	✓	DR	CR
12	2	1580	Oxenford Copperworks	26400	35	26400					
	6	1581	Standard Oil Company	810				644	✔	810	
	7	1582	Khatan Steel Corp.	9900	57	10000	100				
	7	1583	Phoenix Plastics	10486	14	10700	214				
	7	1584	Payroll Bank Account	3420				643	✔	4860	
								214	✔		350
								216	✔		900
								218	✔		190
	9	1585	Scooter Gordon	600				610	✔	600	
	9	1586	Phoenix Plastics	6750	14	6750					
	10	1587	Smith Pipe Company	37719	39	38100	381				
	15	1588	N. Ill. Communications	399				732	✔	399	
	16	1589	Winnebago County Bank	11360				216	✔	9573	
								214	✔	1787	
	16	1590	Phoenix Plastics	52173	14	52700	527				
	20	1591	S. White Trucking	1021				516	✔	1021	
	21	1592	Pen & Pad	1360				125	✔	1360	
	21	1593	Payroll Bank Account	4063				643	✔	5770	
								214	✔		415
								216	✔		1067
								218	✔		225
	22	1594	Business Basics, Inc.	600				151	✔	6100	
								201/16	✔		5500

31

GENERAL LEDGER

ACCOUNT: Cash
101

DATE	EXPLANATION	REF.	DEBIT	CREDIT	BALANCE
2010					
1/1	Balance	✔			3 9 2 1 0
~					~
11/30	Balance	✔			2 0 9 9 3 0

ACCOUNT: Petty Cash
105

DATE	EXPLANATION	REF.	DEBIT	CREDIT	BALANCE
2010					
1/1	Balance	✔			1 5 0

ACCOUNT: Accounts Receivable
112

DATE	EXPLANATION	REF.	DEBIT	CREDIT	BALANCE
2010					
1/1	Balance	✔			1 7 2 6 4 3
~					~
11/30	Balance	✔			3 1 7 4 2 0
12/3		J 9		3 7 0 0	3 1 3 7 2 0
12/15		J 9		4 6 8 0	3 0 9 0 4 0
12/17		J 9		4 5 2 0 0	2 6 3 8 4 0

ACCOUNT: Allowance for Doubtful Accounts   113

DATE	EXPLANATION	REF.	DEBIT	CREDIT	BALANCE
2010					
1/1	Balance	✔			1 3 5 2 0
11/30	Balance	✔			4 5 8 0
12/3		J 9	3 7 0 0		8 8 0

ACCOUNT: Notes Receivable   115

DATE	EXPLANATION	REF.	DEBIT	CREDIT	BALANCE
2010					
1/1	Balance	✔			4 0 0 0 0
11/30	Balance–Platteville Plumbers	✔			4 5 0 0 0
12/17	Bilder Construction	J 9	4 5 2 0 0		9 0 2 0 0

ACCOUNT: Interest Receivable   118

DATE	EXPLANATION	REF.	DEBIT	CREDIT	BALANCE
2010					
1/1	Balance	✔			5 8 0
11/30	Balance	✔			- 0 -

GENERAL LEDGER ACCOUNTS

ACCOUNT: Merchandise Inventory — 120

DATE	EXPLANATION	REF.	DEBIT	CREDIT	BALANCE
2010					
1/1	Balance	✔			5 3 1 9 6 0

ACCOUNT: Office Supplies — 125

DATE	EXPLANATION	REF.	DEBIT	CREDIT	BALANCE
2010					
1/1	Balance	✔			4 7 0
11/30	Balance	✔			2 3 2 0
12/21		CD 18	1 3 6 0		3 6 8 0

ACCOUNT: Prepaid Insurance — 130

DATE	EXPLANATION	REF.	DEBIT	CREDIT	BALANCE
2010					
1/1	Balance	✔			3 9 7 0
11/30	Balance	✔			1 1 0 2 0

ACCOUNT: Prepaid Rent — 131

DATE	EXPLANATION	REF.	DEBIT	CREDIT	BALANCE
2010					
1/1	Balance	✔			3 6 3 0
11/30	Balance	✔			2 5 4 1 0

ACCOUNT: Other Assets   135

DATE	EXPLANATION	REF.		DEBIT	CREDIT	BALANCE
2010						
1/1	Balance	✔				1 3 0 0 0 0
7/1		CD	15	1 5 0 0 0		1 4 5 0 0 0

ACCOUNT: Land   140

DATE	EXPLANATION	REF.	DEBIT	CREDIT	BALANCE
2010					
1/1	Balance	✔			4 3 0 0 0

ACCOUNT: Buildings   145

DATE	EXPLANATION	REF.	DEBIT	CREDIT	BALANCE
2010					
1/1	Balance	✔			3 0 6 0 0 0

GENERAL LEDGER ACCOUNTS

ACCOUNT: Accum. Depr.–Buildings   146

DATE	EXPLANATION	REF.	DEBIT	CREDIT	BALANCE
2010					
1/1	Balance	✔			7 3 0 4 0

ACCOUNT: Office Equipment   151

DATE	EXPLANATION	REF.	DEBIT	CREDIT	BALANCE
2010					
1/1	Balance	✔			3 2 8 0 0
12/22		CD 18	6 1 0 0		3 8 9 0 0

ACCOUNT: Accum. Depr.–Off. Equip.   152

DATE	EXPLANATION	REF.	DEBIT	CREDIT	BALANCE
2010					
1/1	Balance	✔			1 3 2 0 0

ACCOUNT: Delivery Trucks   163

DATE	EXPLANATION	REF.	DEBIT	CREDIT	BALANCE
2010					
1/1	Balance	✔			7 8 4 0 0

ACCOUNT: Accum. Depr.–Delivery Trucks   164

DATE	EXPLANATION	REF.	DEBIT	CREDIT	BALANCE
2010					
1/1	Balance	✔			3 9 5 4 0

ACCOUNT: Notes Payable   200

DATE	EXPLANATION	REF.	DEBIT	CREDIT	BALANCE
2010					
1/1	Balance–renewed 12/31/09	✔			1 5 0 0 0

ACCOUNT: Accounts Payable   201

DATE	EXPLANATION	REF.		DEBIT	CREDIT	BALANCE
2010						
1/1	Balance	✔				8 6 3 5 2
11/30	Balance	✔				1 2 6 8 5 0
12/15		J	9	3 5 5 0		1 2 3 3 0 0
12/22		CD	18		5 5 0 0	1 2 8 8 0 0
12/23		J	9		2 3 0 0	1 3 1 1 0 0

GENERAL LEDGER ACCOUNTS

ACCOUNT: Wages Payable 211

DATE	EXPLANATION	REF.	DEBIT	CREDIT	BALANCE
2010					
1/1	Balance	✔			1906
≈					
11/30	Balance	✔			-0-

ACCOUNT: FICA Taxes Payable 214

DATE	EXPLANATION	REF.	DEBIT	CREDIT	BALANCE
2010					
1/1	Balance	✔			781
≈					
11/30	Balance	✔			1787
12/7		CD 18		350	2137
12/7		J 9		350	2487
12/16		CD 18	1787		700
12/21		J 9		415	1115
12/21		CD 18		415	1530

ACCOUNT: Federal Income Taxes Payable 215

DATE	EXPLANATION	REF.	DEBIT	CREDIT	BALANCE
2010					
1/1	Balance	✔			15789
≈					
11/30	Balance	✔			-0-

GENERAL LEDGER ACCOUNTS

ACCOUNT: Federal Income Tax Withhldg Payable   216

DATE	EXPLANATION	REF.	DEBIT	CREDIT	BALANCE
2010					
1/1	Balance	✔			5148
∫					∫
11/30	Balance	✔			9573
12/7		CD 18		900	10473
12/16		CD 18	9573		900
12/21		CD 18		1067	1967

ACCOUNT: State Income Tax Withhldg Payable   218

DATE	EXPLANATION	REF.	DEBIT	CREDIT	BALANCE
2010					
1/1	Balance	✔			1595
∫					∫
11/30	Balance	✔			2486
12/7		CD 18		190	2676
12/21		CD 18		225	2901

ACCOUNT: Federal Unemployment Taxes Payable   224

DATE	EXPLANATION	REF.	DEBIT	CREDIT	BALANCE
2010					
1/1	Balance	✔			216
∫					∫
11/30	Balance	✔			400

GENERAL LEDGER ACCOUNTS

ACCOUNT: State Unemployment Taxes Payable 226

DATE	EXPLANATION	REF.	DEBIT	CREDIT	BALANCE
2010					
1/1	Balance	✔			1323
11/30	Balance	✔			2600

ACCOUNT: Interest Payable 230

DATE	EXPLANATION	REF.	DEBIT	CREDIT	BALANCE
2010					
1/1	Balance	✔			15165
11/30	Balance	✔			-0-

ACCOUNT: Dividends Payable 250

DATE	EXPLANATION	REF.	DEBIT	CREDIT	BALANCE
2010					
1/1	Balance	✔			23100
11/30	Balance	✔			-0-

ACCOUNT: Notes Payable (LT Liability) 268

DATE	EXPLANATION	REF.	DEBIT	CREDIT	BALANCE
2010					
1/1	Balance	✔			43000
7/1	Increased Mortgage	CR 10		70000	113000

GENERAL LEDGER ACCOUNTS

ACCOUNT: Bonds Payable   270

DATE	EXPLANATION	REF.	DEBIT	CREDIT	BALANCE
2010					
1/1	Balance (issued Mar. 1, 2004)	✔			275000

ACCOUNT: Discount on Bonds Payable   273

DATE	EXPLANATION	REF.	DEBIT	CREDIT	BALANCE
2010					
1/1	Balance	✔			4400

ACCOUNT: Common Stock–$30 Stated Value   311

DATE	EXPLANATION	REF.	DEBIT	CREDIT	BALANCE
2010					
1/1	Balance (6,300 shares)	✔			189000

ACCOUNT: P-I-C in Excess of Stated Value   317

DATE	EXPLANATION	REF.	DEBIT	CREDIT	BALANCE
2010					
1/1	Balance	✔			256400

ACCOUNT: Retained Earnings 320

DATE	EXPLANATION	REF.	DEBIT	CREDIT	BALANCE
2010					
1/1	Balance	✔			3 6 2 7 4 8

ACCOUNT: Treasury Stock-Common 330

DATE	EXPLANATION	REF.	DEBIT	CREDIT	BALANCE
2010					
1/1	Balance (700 shares)	✔			4 4 6 1 0

ACCOUNT: Dividends Declared 333

DATE	EXPLANATION	REF.	DEBIT	CREDIT	BALANCE
2010					

GENERAL LEDGER ACCOUNTS

ACCOUNT: Income Summary   350

DATE	EXPLANATION	REF.	DEBIT	CREDIT	BALANCE
2010					

ACCOUNT: Sales   401

DATE	EXPLANATION	REF.	DEBIT	CREDIT	BALANCE
2010					
11/30	Balance	✔			5 2 3 4 9 4 0

ACCOUNT: Sales Returns and Allowances   412

DATE	EXPLANATION	REF.	DEBIT	CREDIT	BALANCE
2010					
11/30	Balance	✔			9 3 8 0
12/15		J 9	4 6 8 0		1 4 0 6 0

ACCOUNT: Sales Discounts   414

DATE	EXPLANATION	REF.	DEBIT	CREDIT	BALANCE
2010					
11/30	Balance	✔			7 3 0 4 4

GENERAL LEDGER ACCOUNTS

ACCOUNT: Purchases   510

DATE	EXPLANATION	REF.	DEBIT	CREDIT	BALANCE
2010					
11/30	Balance	✔			3 7 2 2 2 9 0

ACCOUNT: Purchases Returns and Allowances   512

DATE	EXPLANATION	REF.		DEBIT	CREDIT	BALANCE
2010						
11/30	Balance	✔				2 5 5 2 0
12/15		J	9		3 5 5 0	2 9 0 7 0

ACCOUNT: Purchases Discounts   514

DATE	EXPLANATION	REF.	DEBIT	CREDIT	BALANCE
2010					
11/30	Balance	✔			6 7 4 9 6

ACCOUNT: Freight-In   516

DATE	EXPLANATION	REF.		DEBIT	CREDIT	BALANCE
2010						
11/30	Balance	✔				1 9 4 4 8
12/20		CD	18	1 0 2 1		2 0 4 6 9
12/23		J	9	2 3 0 0		2 2 7 6 9

ACCOUNT: Advertising Expenses   610

DATE	EXPLANATION	REF.		DEBIT	CREDIT	BALANCE
2010						
11/30	Balance	✔				6578
12/9		CD	18	600		7178

ACCOUNT: Bad Debt Expense   612

DATE	EXPLANATION	REF.	DEBIT	CREDIT	BALANCE
2010					

ACCOUNT: Depreciation Expense–Trucks   617

DATE	EXPLANATION	REF.	DEBIT	CREDIT	BALANCE
2010					

ACCOUNT: Sales Salaries Expense   627

DATE	EXPLANATION	REF.	DEBIT	CREDIT	BALANCE
2010					
11/30	Balance	✔			132990

GENERAL LEDGER ACCOUNTS

ACCOUNT: Wage Expense   643

DATE	EXPLANATION	REF.		DEBIT	CREDIT	BALANCE
2010						
11/30	Balance	✔				110616
12/7		CD	18	4860		115476
12/21		CD	18	5770		121246

ACCOUNT: Freight-Out   644

DATE	EXPLANATION	REF.		DEBIT	CREDIT	BALANCE
2010						
11/30	Balance	✔				17732
12/6		CD	18	810		18542

ACCOUNT: Miscellaneous Selling Expense   649

DATE	EXPLANATION	REF.	DEBIT	CREDIT	BALANCE
2010					

ACCOUNT: Depreciation Expense–Buildings   713

DATE	EXPLANATION	REF.	DEBIT	CREDIT	BALANCE
2010					

ACCOUNT: Depreciation Expense–Off. Equip.   715

DATE	EXPLANATION	REF.	DEBIT	CREDIT	BALANCE
2010					

ACCOUNT: Insurance Expense   722

DATE	EXPLANATION	REF.	DEBIT	CREDIT	BALANCE
2010					

ACCOUNT: Office Salaries Expense   727

DATE	EXPLANATION	REF.	DEBIT	CREDIT	BALANCE
2010					
11/30	Balance	✔			6 8 9 5 1 6

ACCOUNT: Office Supplies Expense   728

DATE	EXPLANATION	REF.	DEBIT	CREDIT	BALANCE
2010					
11/30	Balance	✔			1 5 4 0

GENERAL LEDGER ACCOUNTS

ACCOUNT: Rent Expenses   729

DATE	EXPLANATION	REF.	DEBIT	CREDIT	BALANCE
2010					

ACCOUNT: Payroll Taxes Expense   730

DATE	EXPLANATION	REF.	DEBIT	CREDIT	BALANCE
2010					
11/30	Balance	✔			82916
12/7		J 9	350		83266
12/21		J 9	415		83681

ACCOUNT: Utilities Expense   732

DATE	EXPLANATION	REF.	DEBIT	CREDIT	BALANCE
2010					
11/30	Balance	✔			16270
12/15		CD 18	399		16669

ACCOUNT: Interest Revenue   820

DATE	EXPLANATION	REF.	DEBIT	CREDIT	BALANCE
2010					
11/30	Balance	✔			3150

ACCOUNT: Gain on Plant Assets   826

DATE	EXPLANATION	REF.	DEBIT	CREDIT	BALANCE
2010					

ACCOUNT: Interest Expense   905

DATE	EXPLANATION	REF.	DEBIT	CREDIT	BALANCE
2010					
11/30	Balance	✔			2 4 5 7 0

ACCOUNT: Loss on Plant Asssets   921

DATE	EXPLANATION	REF.	DEBIT	CREDIT	BALANCE
2010					

ACCOUNT: Income Tax Expense 999

DATE	EXPLANATION	REF.	DEBIT	CREDIT	BALANCE
2010					
11/30	Balance	✔			112000

SUBSIDIARY LEDGERS

ACCOUNT: Boecker Builders — 117

DATE	EXPLANATION	REF.	DEBIT	CREDIT	BALANCE
2010					
11/30	Balance	✔			62920
12/9	1050 &	1071		29000	33920
12/13		1071		33920	-0-
12/14		1207	21730		21730

ACCOUNT: The Potts Company — 122

DATE	EXPLANATION	REF.	DEBIT	CREDIT	BALANCE
2010					
11/30	Balance	✔			50300
12/6		1128		50300	-0-
12/13		1206	31450		31450
12/15		1206		4680	26770

ACCOUNT: Swanson Brothers Construction — 133

DATE	EXPLANATION	REF.	DEBIT	CREDIT	BALANCE
2010					
11/30	Balance	✔			24050
12/1		1120		24050	-0-

ACCOUNT: A & B Hardware — 143

DATE	EXPLANATION	REF.	DEBIT	CREDIT	BALANCE
2010					
12/17		1208	7920		7920

ACCOUNTS RECEIVABLE SUBSIDIARY LEDGER

ACCOUNT: Trudy's Plumbing   155

DATE	EXPLANATION	REF.	DEBIT	CREDIT	BALANCE
2010					
11/30	Balance	✔			15100
12/8		1204	26300		41400
12/10		1106		15100	26300
12/10		1205	24850		51150
12/14		1204		26300	24850
12/20		1205		24850	-0-

ACCOUNT: Coconino Contractors, Inc   160

DATE	EXPLANATION	REF.	DEBIT	CREDIT	BALANCE
2010					
11/30	Balance	✔			27800
12/6		1203	10300		38100
12/8		1091		27800	10300
12/20		1209	42780		53080

ACCOUNT: Rankin Plumbing Corp.   166

DATE	EXPLANATION	REF.	DEBIT	CREDIT	BALANCE
2010					
11/30	Balance	✔			74350
12/7		1129		74350	-0-

ACCOUNT: Beverly's Building Products   175

DATE	EXPLANATION	REF.	DEBIT	CREDIT	BALANCE
2010					
11/30	Balance	✔			14000
12/1		1201	13150		27150

ACCOUNT: Bilder Construction Company   180

DATE	EXPLANATION	REF.	DEBIT	CREDIT	BALANCE
2010					
11/30	Balance	✔			45200
12/3		1202	44900		90100
12/17		1120		45200	44900

ACCOUNT: Iwanaga Plumbing and Heating   190

DATE	EXPLANATION	REF.	DEBIT	CREDIT	BALANCE
2010					
11/30	Balance	✔			3700
12/3	Write-Off	780		3700	-0-

ACCOUNT:

DATE	EXPLANATION	REF.	DEBIT	CREDIT	BALANCE
2010					

ACCOUNT:

DATE	EXPLANATION	REF.	DEBIT	CREDIT	BALANCE
2010					

ACCOUNTS PAYABLE SUBSIDIARY LEDGER

ACCOUNT: Phoenix Plastics 14

DATE	EXPLANATION	REF.	DEBIT	CREDIT	BALANCE
2010					
11/30	Balance	✔			17450
12/7		313	10700		6750
12/8	1/10, n/30	316		52700	59450
12/9		299	6750		52700
12/16		316	52700		-0-
12/22	1/10, n/30	319		48330	48330

ACCOUNT: Business Basics, Inc. 16

DATE	EXPLANATION	REF.	DEBIT	CREDIT	BALANCE
2010					
12/22	n/30	318		5500	5500

ACCOUNT: Edward's Plumbing Supplies, Inc. 18

DATE	EXPLANATION	REF.	DEBIT	CREDIT	BALANCE
2010					
11/30	Balance	✔			20050
12/2	n/60	315		24320	44370
12/15		315	3550		40820

ACCOUNT: DeKalb Transport 20

DATE	EXPLANATION	REF.	DEBIT	CREDIT	BALANCE
2010					
12/23	n/30	J9		2300	2300

ACCOUNTS PAYABLE SUBSIDIARY LEDGER

ACCOUNT: Oxenford Copperworks 35

DATE	EXPLANATION	REF.	DEBIT	CREDIT	BALANCE
2010					
11/30	Balance	✔			26400
12/2		280	26400		-0-

ACCOUNT: Smith Pipe Company 39

DATE	EXPLANATION	REF.	DEBIT	CREDIT	BALANCE
2010					
11/30	Balance	✔			38100
12/10		314	38100		-0-
12/17	1/15, n/60	317		43800	43800

ACCOUNT: Ron & Rod's Plumbing Products 44

DATE	EXPLANATION	REF.	DEBIT	CREDIT	BALANCE
2010					
11/30	Balance	✔			14850

ACCOUNT: Khatan Steel Corp. 57

DATE	EXPLANATION	REF.	DEBIT	CREDIT	BALANCE
2010					
11/30	Balance	✔			10000
12/7		312	10000		-0-

ACCOUNTS PAYABLE SUBSIDIARY LEDGER

ACCOUNT: Northern Electric Co.

DATE	EXPLANATION	REF.	DEBIT	CREDIT	BALANCE
2010					

ACCOUNT: City of Rockford

DATE	EXPLANATION	REF.	DEBIT	CREDIT	BALANCE
2010					

TEN-COLUMN WORKSHEET

ACCOUNT TITLES	TRIAL BALANCE		ADJUSTMENTS	
	DR.	CR.	DR.	CR.
Cash				
Petty Cash				
Accounts Receivable				
Allowance for Doubtful Accounts				
Notes Receivable				
Interest Receivable				
Merchandise Inventory				
Office Supplies				
Prepaid Insurance				
Prepaid Rent				
Other Assets				
Land				
Buildings				
Accum. Depr. - Buildings				
Office Equipment				
Accum. Depr. - Off. Equip.				
Delivery Trucks				
Accum. Depr. - Delivery Trucks				
Notes Payable				
Accounts Payable				
Wages Payable				
Salaries Payable				
FICA Taxes Payable				
Federal Income Taxes Payable				
Federal Income Withhldg Tax Payable				
State Income Withhldg Tax Payable				
Federal Unemployment Taxes Pay.				
State Unemployment Taxes Pay.				
Interest Payable				
Dividends Payable				
Notes Payable (LT Liability)				
Bonds Payable				
Discount on Bonds Payable				
Common Stock				
P-I-C in Excess of Stated Value				
Retained Earnings				
Treasury Stock - Common				
Dividends Declared				
Income Summary				
Sales				
Sales Returns and Allowances				
Sales Discounts				
Subtotals				

ADJUSTED TRIAL BALANCE		INCOME STATEMENT		BALANCE SHEET	
DR.	CR.	DR.	CR.	DR.	CR.

ACCOUNT TITLES	TRIAL BALANCE		ADJUSTMENTS	
	DR.	CR.	DR.	CR.
Purchases				
Purchases Returns and Allow.				
Purchases Discounts				
Freight-In				
Advertising Expenses				
Bad Debt Expense				
Depreciation Expense–Trucks				
Sales Salaries Expense				
Wage Expense				
Freight-Out				
Miscellaneous Selling Expense				
Depreciation Expense–Buildings				
Depreciation Expense–Off. Equip.				
Insurance Expense				
Office Salaries Expense				
Office Supplies Expense				
Rent Expenses				
Payroll Taxes Expense				
Utilities Expense				
Interest Revenue				
Gain on Plant Assets				
Interest Expense				
Loss on Plant Assets				
Income Tax Expense				
Totals				
Income Tax Expense				
Federal Income Taxes Payable				
Net Income				
Totals				

ADJUSTED TRIAL BALANCE		INCOME STATEMENT		BALANCE SHEET	
DR.	CR.	DR.	CR.	DR.	CR.

SCHEDULES AND FINANCIAL STATEMENTS

SCHEDULE OF ACCOUNTS RECEIVABLE
SCHEDULE OF ACCOUNTS PAYABLE
INCOME STATEMENT
STATEMENT OF RETAINED EARNINGS
BALANCE SHEET
STATEMENT OF CASH FLOWS
POST-CLOSING TRIAL BALANCE

SCHEDULE OF ACCOUNTS RECEIVABLE
SCHEDULE OF ACCOUNTS PAYABLE

SCHEDULE OF ACCOUNTS RECEIVABLE

SCHEDULE OF ACCOUNTS PAYABLE

Rockford Corporation
Income Statement
For the Year Ended December 31, 2010

Page 1 of 2

69

Rockford Corporation
Statement of Retained Earnings
For the Year Ended December 31, 2010

Rockford Corporation
Balance Sheet
December 31, 2010

Rockford Corporation
Statement of Cash Flows
For the Year Ended December 31, 2010

Rockford Corporation
Post-Closing Trial Balance
December 31, 2010

ROCKFORD CORPORATION

A PRACTICE SET TO ACCOMPANY
Intermediate Accounting, by Kieso, Weygandt, and Warfield

PERPETUAL INVENTORY

Narrative and Instructions

Rockford Corporation is a wholesale plumbing supply distributor. The corporation was organized in 1981, under the laws of the State of Illinois, with an authorized capitalization of 10,000 shares of no-par common stock with a stated value of $30 per share. The common stock is sold over the counter in the local area. You have been hired as of Monday, December 27, 2010, to replace the controller, who has resigned. As controller, you are responsible for the corporation's accounting records, preparation of the financial statements, safeguarding the corporate assets, and providing management with financial information to set prices and to monitor and control operations. You have an assistant who keeps the payroll records, the plant asset ledger, and the perpetual inventory. There is an inventory subsidiary ledger that is posted to daily for purchases and sales. This ledger is not included in this practice set. The corporation secretary maintains the stockholder records, and the receptionist/secretary acts as the petty cashier.

Rockford Corporation closes its books annually on December 31 but prepares financial statements quarterly. Adjusting entries are posted to the general ledger only at year-end; at the end of the first, second, and third quarter the adjustments are entered only on a ten-column work sheet, not in the general ledger. Therefore, *the adjusting entries to be recorded on December 31 are annual adjustments* that you must journalize and then post to the general ledger accounts before preparing the financial statements.

Rockford Corporation maintains a perpetual inventory system and takes a physical count each year to adjust the inventory carrying amount. Purchases are recorded at the gross amount (discounts taken are recognized at the date of payment) of the supplier's invoice, and the terms vary with each supplier. Sales on account are subject to terms of 2/10, n/30. Discounts are taken and granted only when the terms are met. The cost of all inventory sold in December was 80% of the sales price. The corporation uses the following journals and ledgers:

JOURNALS

1. A sales journal (S)–to record sales of merchandise on account.
2. A purchases journal (P)–to record purchases of merchandise on account.
3. A cash receipts journal (CR)–to record all cash receipts.
4. A cash disbursements journal (CD)–to record all cash payments.
5. A general journal (J)–to record all transactions that cannot be recorded in the other journals.

LEDGERS

1. A general ledger.
2. An accounts receivable subsidiary ledger.
3. An accounts payable subsidiary ledger.

In recording sales transactions, each sale should be posted on the day of the sale directly to the customer's account in the subsidiary ledger, using the invoice number as the posting reference number in the subsidiary account. Also, cash receipts from customers should be posted to the subsidiary ledger on the day they are received. The purchase order number should be used as the posting reference number in the subsidiary ledger for purchases on account from suppliers. Purchases from suppliers and payments to them should be posted daily. All other individual posting may be made weekly or at the month-end. Account numbers should be used as posting reference numbers in the journals.

Officers, sales, and office personnel are salaried employees and are paid monthly on the last day of each month. The delivery truck drivers and warehouse employees are hourly wage employees and are paid biweekly. Each biweekly pay period ends Friday. On the following Monday your assistant, who maintains the payroll records, provides you with a payroll summary from which you prepare general journal entries to record the biweekly payroll and the employer's taxes on the payroll. The biweekly employees' paychecks are distributed on the following day (Tuesday).

The general ledger chart of accounts is shown below:

CHART OF ACCOUNTS

Accounts	Account Number
Cash	101
Petty Cash	105
Accounts Receivable	112
Allowance for Doubtful Accounts	113
Notes Receivable	115
Interest Receivable	118
Merchandise Inventory	120
Office Supplies	125
Prepaid Insurance	130
Prepaid Rent	131
Other Assets	135
Land	140
Buildings	145
Accum. Depr.–Buildings	146
Office Equipment	151
Accum. Depr.–Off. Equip.	152
Delivery Trucks	163
Accum. Depr.–Delivery Trucks	164
Notes Payable	200
Accounts Payable	201
Wages Payable	211
Salaries Payable	212
FICA Taxes Payable	214
Federal Income Taxes Payable	215
Federal Income Tax Withholding Payable	216
State Income Tax Withholding Payable	218
Federal Unemployment Taxes Payable	224
State Unemployment Taxes Payable	226
Interest Payable	230
Dividends Payable	250
Notes Payable (LT Liability)	268
Bonds Payable	270
Discount on Bonds Payable	273
Common Stock	311
P-I-C in Excess of Stated Value	317
Retained Earnings	320
Treasury Stock-Common	330
Dividends Declared	333
Income Summary	350
Sales	401
Sales Returns and Allowances	412
Sales Discounts	414
Cost of Goods Sold	505
Advertising Expenses	610
Bad Debt Expense	612
Depreciation Expense-Trucks	617
Sales Salaries Expense	627
Wage Expense	643
Freight-out	644
Miscellaneous Selling Expense	649
Depreciation Expense–Buildings	713
Depreciation Expense–Off. Equip.	715
Insurance Expense	722
Office Salaries Expense	727
Office Supplies Expense	728
Rent Expenses	729
Payroll Taxes Expense	730
Utilities Expense	732
Interest Revenue	820
Gain on Plant Assets	826
Interest Expense	905
Loss on Plant Assets	921
Income Tax Expense	999

The January 1, 2010, balances appear in the general ledger accounts as well as the November 30, 2010, balances, for those accounts whose balances have changed. All transactions affecting the noncurrent accounts from January 1, 2010, through November 30, 2010, with explanations, appear in these accounts to facilitate the preparation of the statement of cash flows.

Subsidiary ledger account balances as of November 30, 2010, are as follows (the balances appear in the appropriate subsidiary ledger accounts):

ACCOUNTS RECEIVABLE

Boecker Builders	$62,920
The Potts Company	50,300
Swanson Brothers Construction	24,050
Trudy's Plumbing	15,100
Coconino Contractors, Inc.	27,800
Rankin Plumbing Corp.	74,350
Beverly's Building Products	14,000
Bilder Construction Company	45,200
Iwanaga Plumbing and Heating	3,700
Total accounts receivable	$317,420

ACCOUNTS PAYABLE

Phoenix Plastics	$17,450

Edward's Plumbing Supplies, Inc.	20,050
Oxenford Copperworks	26,400
Smith Pipe Company	38,100
Ron & Rod's Plumbing Products	14,850
Khatan Steel Corp.	10,000
Total accounts payable	$126,850

The transactions through December 23 have already been recorded by the former controller. You are to begin your work by entering the transaction of December 27 for the payment of cash to repurchase stock.

DECEMBER 2010

S	M	T	W	T	F	S
			1	2	3	4
5	6	7	8	9	10	11
12	13	14	15	16	17	18
19	20	21	22	23	24	25
26	27	28	29	30	31	

NARRATIVE OF THE DECEMBER TRANSACTIONS

NOTE: All transactions from Dec. 1 thru Dec. 23
have already been recorded

December

1   Received a check in the amount of $23,569 from Swanson Brothers Construction in full payment of invoice No. 1120 dated November 26 in the amount of $24,050.

1   Sold sewer and drainage pipe to Beverly's Building Products on account, invoice No. 1201 for $13,150.

2   Purchased copper tubing and fittings from Edward's Plumbing Supplies Inc. on account, purchase order No. 315 for $24,320, terms n/60.

2   Issued check No. 1580 for $26,400 to Oxenford Copperworks in settlement of the balance owed on purchase order No. 280.

3   A court notice indicates that Iwanaga Plumbing and Heating is bankrupt and payment of its account improbable; the president orders the account to be written off as a bad debt (invoice No. 780).

3   Sold bathroom fixtures to Bilder Construction Company on account, invoice No.1202 for $44,900.

6   Received a check in the amount of $49,294 from The Potts Company in full payment of invoice No. 1128 dated November 27 for $50,300.

6   Sold plumbing supplies and plastic pipe to Coconino Contractors, Inc. on account, invoice No. 1203 for $10,300.

6   Issued check No. 1581 for $810 to Standard Oil Co. in payment of gas, oil, and truck repair from Tierney's Standard Service.

7   Issued check No. 1582 for $9,900 to Khatan Steel Corp. in full settlement of purchase order No. 312 for $10,000.

7   Issued check No. 1583 for $10,486 to Phoenix Plastics in full payment of Phoenix's invoice dated November 28 in the amount of $10,700, for purchase order No. 313, terms 2/10, n/30.

7   Received a check in the amount of $72,863 from Rankin Plumbing Corp. in full payment of invoice No. 1129 dated November 28 for $74,350.

7   The payroll summary for the biweekly pay period ended Friday, December 3 contained the following information:

Delivery and warehouse wages	$4,860
FICA taxes withheld	350
Federal income taxes withheld	900
State income taxes withheld	190
Net pay	$3,420
Employer's payroll taxes:	
FICA tax	$ 350
Federal unemployment tax	–
State unemployment tax	–

Issued check No. 1584 for the amount of the net pay and deposited it in the payroll bank account. Individual payroll checks were then prepared for distribution to the biweekly employees on Tuesday, December 7.

8 Sold cast pipe to Trudy's Plumbing on account, invoice No. 1204 for $26,300.

8 Received a check in the amount of $27,800 from Coconino Contractors, Inc. in full payment of invoice No. 1091 dated October 20.

8 Purchased bathroom fixtures from Phoenix Plastics, on account, purchase order No. 316 for $52,700 terms 1/10, n/30.

9 Issued check No. 1585 for $600 to Scooter Gordon for lettering and sign painting on some delivery trucks.

9 Received a check in the amount of $29,000 from Boecker Builders in partial payment of balance outstanding covering invoice Nos. 1050 and 1071.

9 Issued check No. 1586 for $6,750 to Phoenix Plastics, in payment of Phoenix's invoice dated November 12 in the amount of $6,750, our purchase order No. 299.

10 Issued check No. 1587 for $37,719 to Smith Pipe Company in full payment of their invoice dated November 28, terms 1/15, n/60, our purchase order No. 314.

10 Received a check in the amount of $15,100 from Trudy's Plumbing in full settlement of invoice No. 1106 dated November 7.

10 Sold pipe, fixtures, and accessories to Trudy's Plumbing on account, invoice No. 1205 for $24,850.

13 Sold plumbing supplies and copper tubing to The Potts Company on account, invoice No. 1206 for $31,450

13 Received a check in the amount of $33,920 from Boecker Builders in full payment of invoice No. 1071.

13 Cash sales to date totaled $12,292.

14 Received a check in the amount of $25,774 from Trudy's Plumbing in payment of invoice No. 1204.

14 Sold plumbing fixtures and supplies to Boecker Builders, on account, invoice No. 1207 for $21,730.

15 The Potts Company returned defective copper tubing that it purchased on December 10. A credit memo in the amount of $4,680 is issued relative to invoice No. 1206. The copper tubing had a cost of $3,550.

15 The defective copper tubing is returned to Edward's Plumbing Supplies, Inc. along with a debit memo in the amount of $3,550 in reduction of purchase order No. 315.

15 Issued check No. 1588 for $399 in payment of November telephone bill to Northern Illinois Communications.

16 Issued check No. 1589 in the amount of $11,360 in payment of federal withholding taxes, $9,573, and FICA taxes, $1,787, payable on November salaries and wages; the check is remitted to the Winnebago County Bank as the depository.

16 Issued check No. 1590 for $52,173 to Phoenix Plastics, Inc. in payment of purchase order No. 316.

17 The president informs you that Bilder Construction Company agrees to convert the $45,200 overdue account receivable (invoice No. 1120) to a 14% note due six months from today.

17 Purchased plumbing materials from Smith Pipe Company on account, purchase order No. 317 for $43,800 terms 1/15, n/60.

17 Sold drain tile, plastic pipe, and copper tubing to A & B Hardware on account, invoice No. 1208 for $7,920.

20 Sold fixtures and materials to Coconino Contractors, Inc. on account, invoice No. 1209 for $42,780.

20 An invoice in the amount of $1,021 was received from S. White Trucking Company for freight on purchase order No. 317 and paid by issuing check No. 1591.

20 Received a check in the amount of $24,353 from Trudy's Plumbing in payment of invoice No. 1205.

21 Purchased office supplies from the Pen & Pad, issuing check No. 1592 in the amount of $1,360. (Note: Debit asset account).

21 The payroll summary for the biweekly pay period ended Friday, December 17, contained the following information:

Delivery and warehouse wages	$5,770
FICA taxes withheld	415
Federal income taxes withheld	1,067
State income taxes withheld	225
Net pay	$4,063
Employer's payroll taxes:	
FICA tax	$ 415
Federal unemployment tax	–
State unemployment tax	–

Issued check No. 1593 for the amount of the net pay and deposited it in the payroll bank account. Individual payroll checks were then prepared for distribution to the biweekly employees on Tuesday, December 21.

22 Purchased a new Faith computer for $6,100 from Business Basics, Inc., purchase order No. 318, paying $600 down through Check No. 1594 with the balance due in thirty days (n/30). The computer has an estimated life of five years with a salvage value of $1,300. Use subsidiary account No. 16. Journalize the entire entry in the cash disbursements journal.

22 Purchased bathroom and kitchen fixtures from Phoenix Plastics, on account, purchase order No. 319 for $48,330, terms 1/10, n/30.

23 Received a bill from DeKalb Transport for $2,300 for freight costs incurred during the last 30 days, terms n/30.

NOTE: Transactions up to this point have been recorded. At this point you became controller and are responsible for recording all further transactions.

√27 The board of directors voted to purchase 1,000 shares of its own stock from stockholder Dionne Schivone at $83 per share and issued check No. 1595 in payment. Stock repurchases are recorded at cost. Rockford is purchasing these shares because Ms. Schivone had been a valuable employee.

√27 The board of directors declared a $2.70 per-share cash dividend payable on January 14 to stockholders of record on December 27 (after purchase of stock).

√27 The president informs you that Beverly's Building Products agrees to convert the $14,000 overdue accounts receivable (invoice No. 1119) balance to a 12% note due six months from today.

√28 A half-acre parcel of land adjacent to the building is acquired in exchange for 600 shares of unissued common stock. The land has a fair value of $54,000 and will be used immediately as an outside storage lot and parking lot.

√28 An invoice in the amount of $2,650 is received from Wayne McManus, lawyer, for legal services involved in the acquisition of the adjacent parcel of land; check No. 1596 is issued in payment.

√28 Sold pipe and plumbing materials to Boecker Builders on account, invoice No. 1210 for $42,040.

√29 Issued check No. 1597 in the amount of $500 to the *Northern Star* for advertisement run in the home building supplement of December 13.

√29 Issued check No. 1598 in the amount of $925 to Standard Oil Co. in payment of gas, oil, and truck repairs from Standard Oil Co. (use Freight-out).

√29 Purchased copper and cast iron pipe from Oxenford Copperworks on account, purchase order No. 320 for $55,940, terms 1/10, n/30.

√29 Check No. 1599 for $15,000 is issued to the bond sinking fund trustee, Chicago Trust Co., for deposit in the sinking fund. (Use Other Assets).

√30 Received a check for $21,730 from Boecker Builders in payment of invoice No. 1207.

√30 Sold plumbing supplies to Swanson Brothers Construction on account, invoice No. 1211 for $24,650.

√30 Issued check No. 1600 for $43,362 to Smith Pipe Company in payment of purchase order No. 317.

√31 The custodian of the petty cash fund submits the following receipts for reimbursement and reports a cash-on-hand count of $8.

Postage stamps used	$38
United Parcel (freight-out)	23
C.O.D. postage (freight costs)	51
Christmas office decorations	30

Check No. 1601 is issued and cashed to reimburse the fund.

√31 Sold an electric truck-lift to Leila Stierman Co. for $2,500 cash. The original cost was $7,900 with salvage value of $900, a life of 10 years, and accumulated depreciation recorded through 12/31/09 of $4,550. The straight-line method is used. (Note: the company follows the practice of recording a half year's depreciation in the year of acquisition and a half year in the year of disposal.) First, bring the depreciation expense up to date in the general journal. Then journalize the entire entry for the sale in the cash receipts journal.

√31 Sold bathroom fixtures and plumbing supplies to Trudy's Plumbing on account, invoice No. 1212 for $55,770.

√31 Because for some time the petty cash fund has been smaller than required for monthly expenditures, the fund is increased by $75 by cashing check No. 1602 and placing the money in the petty cash fund.

√31 The payroll summary for the *monthly* paid employees is submitted so that December checks can be distributed before the year-end; the details are as follows:

Sales salaries	$16,000
Office and administrative salaries.........................	22,900
Federal income taxes withheld	7,196
State income taxes withheld	1,517
FICA taxes withheld..	2,120
Net pay...	$28,067

Issued check No. 1603 for the amount of the net pay and deposited it in the payroll bank account. Individual payroll checks were prepared for distribution to all monthly employees by the end of the day.

Employer's payroll taxes:	
FICA tax (all office and administrative)..........	$2,120
Federal unemployment tax..............................	–
State unemployment tax.................................	–

31 Cash sales since December 13 total $25,980.

INSTRUCTIONS

1. Make the entries in the appropriate journals for December 27 through December 31.

2. Post any amounts to be posted as individual amounts from the journals to the general ledger and any amounts to be posted to the subsidiary ledger accounts. (If the normal practice of daily posting were followed, the postings would be in chronological order; proper date sequence for this practice set is not necessary.)

3. Foot and cross-foot the columnar journals and complete the month-end postings of all books of original entry.

4. Prepare a trial balance by entering the account balances from the general ledger in the first two columns of the ten-column work sheet (list all accounts, including those with zero balances).

5. From the following information prepare adjusting entries in the general journal and enter them in the "adjustments" columns of the work sheet and cross-reference the amounts using the related alphabetic characters (round all calculations to the nearest dollar).

a. The annual provision for doubtful accounts receivable is recorded by providing a charge to Bad Debt Expense in an amount equal to 2% of net sales. (This entry should be entered below the middle of General Journal page 10.)

b. An inventory count of the office supplies revealed $830 of supplies on hand at year-end.

c. The insurance premium outstanding on January 1, 2010, covers the period January 1 through August 31, 2010. The insurance premium of $7,050 recorded in August covers the period of September 1, 2010 through August 31, 2011. Rockford estimates that 75% of the premiums are attributable to general activities and 25% to selling activities. (Use Miscellaneous Selling Expense).

d. The payroll summary for the employees who are paid biweekly shows the following information at December 31, 2010:

Delivery and Warehouse Wages	$5,600
FICA Taxes Payable	375
Federal Withholding Taxes	1,036
State Withholding Taxes...	218
Net pay...	$3,971

e. The employer's share of the FICA tax ($375) must be accrued; no state or federal unemployment tax is incurred during the fourth quarter because all wages and salaries earned during the last quarter exceed the maximum subject to unemployment tax.

f. Interest has accrued at 8% on the long-term notes payable since July 1, 2010. The next six-month interest payment at 9% on the bonds is due on March 1, 2011. The discount on bonds payable has not been amortized for any part of 2010; the bonds are dated March 1, 2004, and mature March 1, 2014. (Use straight-line.)

g. The interest accrued to 12/31/10 on notes receivable is composed of the following:

Platteville Plumbers, 10%, 6 months, due March 31, 2011	$1,125
Bilder Construction, 11%, 6 months, due June 14, 2011	232
Beverly's Building, 9%, 6 months, due June 26, 2011	17
	$1,374

The interest accrued at 12/31/10 on the note payable of $15,000 @ 10% is $1,500. Interest is payable on January 2, 2011. (The note is due in 2011.)

h. A warehouse lease payment of $10,890 was made on September 1, 2010, for rental through February 28, 2011. (The Prepaid Rent account is for advance lease payments on the warehouse.)

i. $530 is owed to Northern Electric Co. and $279 is owed to City of Rockford for utility services provided during December 2010.

j. Plant and equipment to be depreciated are composed of the following:

Assets	Date Acquired	Cost	Estimated Usage or Life	Salvage Value	Depreciation Method
Building	7/1/06	$306,000	25 years	$20,000	sum-of-the-years' digits
Truck No. 1	4/1/07	28,000	60,000 miles	3,100	miles driven
Truck No. 2	9/1/09	33,000	60,000 miles	4,200	miles driven
Lift No. 1 (Sold 12/31/10)	8/17/03	7,900	10 years	900	straight-line
Lift No. 2	3/29/07	4,500	10 years	500	straight-line
Lift No. 3	9/16/08	5,000	10 years	500	straight-line
Office Equipment	All prior to 1/1/10	32,800	7 years	2,000	straight-line
Computer	12/22/10	6,100	5 years	1,300	Double-decling balance

Truck No. 1 has been driven 45,000 miles prior to 1/1/10 and truck No. 2 has been driven 30,500 miles prior to 1/1/10. During 2010 truck No. 1 was driven 12,000 miles and truck No. 2 was driven 14,000 miles. Remember that the Rockford Company takes a half-year's depreciation in the year of acquisition and a half-year in the year of sale.

6. Complete the work sheet. In completing the worksheet, compute State of Illinois corporate income taxes at 4½% of pretax income. The state income tax is deductible on the federal tax return, and the federal tax is *not* deductible on the Illinois return. Assume federal corporate income tax on income subject to federal tax is as follows:

first $50,000	@15%
next 25,000	@25%
remainder	@34%

Income between $100,000 and $335,000 is assessed a 5% federal surtax, not to exceed $11,750.

Hint: Corporations subject to federal income tax must make estimated tax payments throughout the year. At the time of the payment, the account Income Tax Expense is debited and Cash is credited. To determine the taxable income at year end, net the total debits and total credits from the income statement in the worksheet. Note that the estimated income tax expense is listed as a debit and must be subtracted from total debits when determining taxable income (federal tax is not a deductible item).

7. Prepare the journal entry for income taxes. Post all adjusting entries.

8. Prepare schedules of subsidiary accounts receivable and accounts payable and determine that the total per each subsidiary schedule agrees with the related control account.

9. Prepare an income statement (assume the weighted-average number of shares outstanding for the year 2010 is 5,600 shares). Assume that bad debt expense is an administrative expense. Assure payroll taxes expense is 80% administrative.

10. Prepare a statement of retained earnings.

11. Prepare a balance sheet. (Hint: combine Petty Cash with Cash for balance sheet purposes.)

12. *OPTIONAL ASSIGNMENT* (1 to 1½ hours): Prepare a statement of cash flows using the indirect approach. (Hint: combine Petty Cash with Cash for purposes of determining changes in cash.)

13. Prepare and post closing entries.

14. Prepare a post-closing trial balance.

AN ALTERNATIVE SET OF INSTRUCTIONS
FOR ROCKFORD CORPORATION

To the Student: These pages contain a second set of instructions which, if assigned by the instructor, are to be utilized in place of pages 84-86. The primary differences between these two sets are in the adjusting entries, instruction steps 5 through 9. All other information, forms, and requirements are the same.

ALTERNATIVE SET OF INSTRUCTIONS

1. Make the entries in the appropriate journals for December 27 through December 31.

2. Post any amounts to be posted as individual amounts from the journals to the general ledger and any amounts to be posted to the subsidiary ledger accounts. (If the normal practice of daily posting were followed, the postings would be in chronological order; proper date sequence for this practice set is not necessary.)

3. Foot and cross-foot the columnar journals and complete the month-end postings of all books of original entry.

4. Prepare a trial balance by entering the account balances from the general ledger in the first two columns of the ten-column work sheet (list all accounts, including those with zero balances).

5. From the following information prepare adjusting entries in the general journal and enter them in the "adjustments" columns of the work sheet and cross-reference the amounts using the related alphabetic characters (round all calculations to the nearest dollar).

    a. The annual provision for doubtful accounts receivable is recorded by providing a charge to Bad Debt Expense in an amount equal to $1\frac{1}{2}\%$ of net sales. (This entry should be entered below the middle of General Journal page 10.)

    b. An inventory count of the office supplies revealed $810 of supplies on hand at year-end.

    c. The insurance premium outstanding on January 1, 2010, covers the period January 1 through August 31, 2010. The insurance premium of $7,050 recorded in August covers the period of September 1, 2010 through August 31, 2011. Rockford estimates that 80% of the premiums are attributable to general activities and 20% to selling activities. (Use Miscellaneous Selling Expense).

    d. The payroll summary for the employees who are paid biweekly shows the following information at December 31, 2010:

Delivery and Warehouse Wages	$5,300
FICA Taxes Payable	360
Federal Withholding Taxes	980
State Withholding Taxes	200
Net pay	$3,760

e. The employer's share of the FICA tax ($360) must be accrued; no state or federal unemployment tax is incurred during the fourth quarter because all wages and salaries earned during the last quarter exceed the maximum subject to unemployment tax.

f. Interest has accrued at 9% on the long-term notes payable since July 1, 2010. The next six-month interest payment at 9% on the bonds is due on March 1, 2011. The discount on bonds payable has not been amortized for any part of 2010; the bonds are dated March 1, 2004, and mature March 1, 2014.

g. The interest accrued to 12/31/10 on notes receivable is composed of the following:

Platteville Plumbers, 11%, 6 months, due March 31, 211	$1,237
Bilder Construction, 10%, 6 months, due June 14, 2011	211
Beverly's Building, 9%, 6 months, due June 26, 2011	17
	$1,465

The interest accrued at 12/31/10 on the note payable of $15,000 @ 10% is $1,500. Interest is payable on January 2, 2011.

h. A warehouse lease payment of $10,890 was made on September 1, 2010, for rental through February 28, 2011. (The Prepaid Rent account is for advance lease payments on the warehouse.)

i. $590 is owed to Northern Electric Co. and $270 is owed to City of Rockford for utility services provided during December 2010.

j. Plant and equipment to be depreciated are composed of the following:

Assets	Date Acquired	Cost	Estimated Usage or Life	Salvage Value	Depreciation Method
Building	7/1/06	$306,000	25 years	$20,000	sum-of-the-years' digits
Truck No. 1	4/1/07	28,000	60,000 miles	3,100	miles driven
Truck No. 2	9/1/09	33,000	60,000 miles	4,200	miles driven
Lift No. 1 (Sold 12/31/10)	8/17/03	7,900	10 years	900	straight-line
Lift No. 2	3/29/07	4,500	10 years	500	straight-line
Lift No. 3	9/16/08	5,000	10 years	500	straight-line
Office Equipment	All prior to 1/1/10	32,800	7 years	2,000	straight-line
Computer	12/22/10	6,100	6 years	1,300	Double-decling balance

Truck No. 1 has been driven 45,000 miles prior to 1/1/10 and truck No. 2 has been driven 30,500 miles prior to 1/1/10. During 2010 truck No. 1 was driven 15,000 miles and truck No. 2 was driven 12,000 miles. Remember that the Rockford Company takes a half-year's depreciation in the year of acquisition and a half-year in the year of sale.

6. Complete the work sheet. In completing the worksheet, compute State of Illinois corporate income taxes at 4% of pretax income. The state income tax is deductible on the federal tax return, and the federal tax is *not* deductible on the Illinois return. Assume federal corporate income tax on income subject to federal tax is as follows:

first $50,000	@15%
next 25,000	@25%
remainder	@34%

Income between $100,000 and $335,000 is assessed a 5% federal surtax, not to exceed $11,750.

Hint: Corporations subject to federal income tax must make estimated tax payments throughout the year. At the time of the payment, the account Income Tax Expense is debited and Cash is credited. To determine the taxable income at year end, net the total debits and total credits from the income statement in the worksheet. Note that the estimated income tax expense is listed as a debit and must be subtracted from total debits when determining taxable income (federal tax is not a deductible item).

7. Prepare the journal entry for income taxes. Post all adjusting entries.

8. Prepare schedules of subsidiary accounts receivable and accounts payable and determine that the total per each subsidiary schedule agrees with the related control account.

9. Prepare an income statement (assume the weighted-average number of shares outstanding for the year 2010 is 5,592 shares). Assume that bad debt expense is an administrative expense. Assume payroll taxes expense is 80% administrative.

10. Prepare a statement of retained earnings.

11. Prepare a balance sheet. (Hint: combine Petty Cash with Cash for balance sheet purposes.)

12. *OPTIONAL ASSIGNMENT* (1 to 1½ hours): Prepare a statement of cash flows using the indirect approach. (Hint: combine Petty Cash with Cash for purposes of determining changes in cash.)

13. Prepare and post closing entries.

14. Prepare a post-closing trial balance.

JOURNALS

GENERAL JOURNAL
PURCHASES JOURNAL
SALES JOURNAL
CASH RECEIPTS JOURNAL
CASH DISBURSEMENTS JOURNAL

DATE 2010		Account Titles and Explanation	REF.	DEBIT	CREDIT
12	3	Allowance for Doubtful Accounts	113	3 7 0 0	
		Accounts Receivable–Iwanaga Plumbing and Heating	112/190		3 7 0 0
		To record the write-off of an			
		account due to bankruptcy.			
12	7	Payroll Taxes Expense	730	3 5 0	
		FICA Taxes Payable	214		3 5 0
		To record employer's portion of			
		FICA taxes on biweekly payroll.			
12	15	Sales Returns and Allowances	412	4 6 8 0	
		Accounts Receivable–The Potts Company	112/122		4 6 8 0
		To record defective copper tubing returned			
		by customer.			
		Merchandise Inventory	120	3 5 5 0	
		Cost of Goods Sold	505		3 5 5 0
		To record cost of goods returned by customer			
12	15	Accounts Payable–Edward's Plumbing Supplies, Inc.	201/18	3 5 5 0	
		Merchandise Inventory	120		3 5 5 0
		To record defective copper tubing returned			
		to supplier.			
12	17	Notes Receivable	115	4 5 2 0 0	
		Accounts Receivable–Bilder Construction	112/180		4 5 2 0 0
		To record receipt of a 14%, 6-month			
		note for an overdue accounts receivable			
12	21	Payroll Taxes Expense	730	4 1 5	
		FICA Taxes Payable	214		4 1 5
		To record employer's portion of			
		FICA taxes on biweekly payroll			
12	23	Merchandise Inventory	120	2 3 0 0	
		Accounts Payable–DeKalb Transport	201/20		2 3 0 0
		To record freight costs for December, 2010.			

DATE 2010		Account Titles and Explanation	REF.	DEBIT	CREDIT
			140	5 4 0 00	
			311		1 8 0 00
			317		3 6 0 00
			617	4 5 0	
			164		4 5 0
ADJUSTING ENTRIES AT 12/31/10					
12	31	Bad Debt Expense	618	1 1 0 5 5 9	
		Allowance for Doubtful Account	113		1 1 0 5 5 9
		2% of Net Sales (5527951 x 2%)			
12	31	Office Supplies Expense	727	2 8 5 0	
		Office Supplies	125		2 8 5 0
		Correct Balance to whats on hand			
12	31	Insurance Expense	722	1 7 6 3	
		Miscellaneous Selling Expense	649	5 8 7	
		Prepaid Insurance	130		2 3 5 0
		Correct Insurance used from 9/1 - 12/31			

DATE 2010		Account Titles and Explanation	REF.	DEBIT	CREDIT
12	31	Wage Expense	643	5600	
		FICA Taxes Payable	214		375
		Federal Income Tax Withhldg Payable	216		1036
		State Income Tax Withhldg Payable	218		218
		Wages Payable	211		3971
		Record bi-weekly payroll through 12/31			
12	31	Payroll Tax Expense	730	375	
		FICA Taxes Payable	214		375
		Employer Portion of FICA Taxes bi-weekly payroll			
12	31	Interest Expense	905	4520	
		Interest Payable	230		4520
		Record Interest on Long Term Liabilities 7/1-12/31			
12	31	Bond Interest Expense	905	25630	
		Bond Interest Payable	230		24750
		Discount on Bonds Payable	273		880
		Record Interest on Bonds for 6 months			
12	31	Interest Expense	905	1500	
		Interest Payable	230		1500
		Record Interest on Notes Payable			
12	31	Rent Expense	729	7260	
		Prepaid Rent	131		7260
		Rent Used from 9/1-12/31			
12	31	Utilities Expense	732	809	
		Accounts Payable-Northern Electric Co.	201/		536
		Accounts Payable - City of Rockford	201/		279
		Record Utilities for 12/31/10			
12	31	Depreciation Expense - Buildings	713	4400	
		Accumulated Depreciation- Buildings	146		4400
		Record Depreciation of Buildings			
12	31	Depreciation Expense - Off. Equip	715	4400	
		Accumulated Depreciation-Off. Equip.	152		4400
		Record Depreciation of Office Equipment			
12	31	Depreciation Expense - Delivery Trucks	617	6640	
		Accumulated Depreciation-Delivery Trucks	164		6640
		Record Depreciation of Delivery Truck #1			

DATE 2010		Account Titles and Explanation	REF.	DEBIT	CREDIT
12	31	Depreciation Expense - Off. Equip.	715	1 2 0 3	
		Accumulated Depreciation - Off. Equip.	152		2 0 3
		Record Depreciation for Computer			
12	31	Depreciation Expense - Delivery Trucks	617	1 3 2 2 0	
		Accumulated Depreciation - Delivery Trucks	164		1 3 2 2 0
		Record Depreciation of Delivery Truck #2			
12	31	Depreciation Expense - Delivery Trucks	617	4 0 0	
		Accumulated Depreciation - Delivery Trucks	164		4 0 0
		Record Depreciation of Lift #2			
12	31	Depreciation Expense - Delivery Trucks	617	4 5 0	
		Accumulated Depreciation - Delivery Trucks	164		4 5 0
		Record Depreciation of Lift #3			
12	31	Income Tax Expense	999	2 2 6 6 9	
		Federal Income Tax Payable	215		2 2 6 6 9

DATE 2010		Account Titles and Explanation	REF.	DEBIT	CREDIT
CLOSING ENTRIES AT 12/31/10					
12	31	Sales	401	5619052	
		Income Summary	350		5619052
12	31	Income Summary	350	14060	
		Sales Returns and Allowances	412		14060
12	31	Income Summary	350	77041	
		Sales Discounts	414		77041
12	31	Interest Revenue	820	3150	
		Income Summary	350		3150
12	31	Income Summary	350	3952462	
		Cost of Goods Sold	505		3952462
12	31	Income Summary	350	400	
		Loss on Plant Assets	921		400

DATE 2010		Account Titles and Explanation	REF.	DEBIT	CREDIT
12	31	Income Summary	350	1422684	
		Advertising Expense	610		7678
		Bad Debt Expense	612		110559
		Depreciation Expense -Trucks	617		21160
		Sales Salaries Expense	627		148990
		Wage Expense	643		126846
		Freight - Out	644		19541
		Miscellaneous Selling Expense	649		587
		Depreciation Expense - Buildings	713		4400
		Depreciation Expense - Off. Equip.	715		4603
		Insurance Expense	722		1763
		Office Salaries Expense	727		712416
		Office Supplies Expense	728		4458
		Rent Expenses	729		7260
		Payroll Taxes Expense	730		84056
		Utilities Expense	732		17478
		Interest Expense	905		56220
		Income Tax Expense	999		94669
12	31	Income Summary	350	155555	
		Retained Earnings	320		155555
12	31	Retained Earnings	320	14310	
		Dividends Declared	333		14310

DATE 2010		PUR. ORDER NO.	ACCOUNT CREDITED	ACCT. NO.	AMOUNT	
12	2	315	Edward's Plumbing Supplies, Inc. n/60	18	24	320
	8	316	Phoenix Plastics 1/10, n/30	14	52	700
	17	317	Smith Pipe Company 1/15, n/60	39	43	800
	22	318	(see Cash Disbursements Journal)			
	22	319	Phoenix Plastics 1/10, n/30	14	48	330

DATE 2010		INVOICE NO.	ACCOUNT DEBITED	ACCT. NO.	ACCT. REC. DR SALES CR			COST OF GOODS SOLD DR MER. INVEN. CR		
12	1	1201	Beverly's Building Products	175	13	150		10	520	
	3	1202	Bilder Construction Co.	180	44	900		35	920	
	6	1203	Coconino Contractors, Inc.	160	10	300		8	240	
	8	1204	Trudy's Plumbing	155	26	300		21	040	
	10	1205	Trudy's Plumbing	155	24	850		19	880	
	13	1206	The Potts Company	122	31	450		25	160	
	14	1207	Boecker Builders	117	21	730		17	384	
	17	1208	A & B Hardware	143	7	920		6	336	
	20	1209	Coconino Contractors, Inc.	160	42	780		34	224	

DATE 2010		DESCRIPTION	CASH DR	SALES DISCOUNTS DR	REF	ACCOUNTS RECEIVABLE CR	SALES CR	SUNDRY ACCOUNTS			
								ACCT. NO.	✓	DR	CR
12	1	Swanson Brothers Construction	23569	481	133	24050					
	6	The Potts Company	49294	1006	122	50300					
	7	Rankin Plumbing Corp.	72863	1487	166	74350					
	8	Coconino Contractors, Inc.	27800		160	27800					
	9	Boecker Builders	29000		117	29000					
	10	Trudy's Plumbing	15100		155	15100					
	13	Boecker Builders	33920		117	33920					
	13	Cash sales	12292				12292				
								505	✔	9834	
								120	✔		9834
	14	Trudy's Plumbing	25774	526	155	26300					
	20	Trudy's Plumbing	24353	497	155	24850					

DATE 2010		CHECK NO.	PAYEE	CASH CR	REF	ACCOUNTS PAYABLE DR	MERCHAN. INVENTORY CR	SUNDRY ACCOUNTS ACCT NO.	✔	DR	CR
12	2	1580	Oxenford Copperworks	26400	35	26400					
	6	1581	Standard Oil Company	810				644	✔	810	
	7	1582	Khatan Steel Corp.	9900	57	10000	100				
	7	1583	Phoenix Plastics	10486	14	10700	214				
	7	1584	Payroll Bank Account	3420				643	✔	4860	
								214	✔		350
								216	✔		900
								218	✔		190
	9	1585	Scooter Gordon	600				610	✔	600	
	9	1586	Phoenix Plastics	6750	14	6750					
	10	1587	Smith Pipe Company	37719	39	38100	381				
	15	1588	N. Ill. Communications	399				732	✔	399	
	16	1589	Winnebago County Bank	11360				216	✔	9573	
								214	✔	1787	
	16	1590	Phoenix Plastics	52173	14	52700	527				
	20	1591	S. White Trucking	1021				120	✔	1021	
	21	1592	Pen & Pad	1360				125	✔	1360	
	21	1593	Payroll Bank Account	4063				643	✔	5770	
								214	✔		415
								216	✔		1067
								218	✔		225
	22	1594	Business Basics, Inc.	600				151	✔	6100	
								201/16	✔		5500

GENERAL LEDGER

GENERAL LEDGER ACCOUNTS

ACCOUNT: Cash   101

DATE	EXPLANATION	REF.	DEBIT	CREDIT	BALANCE
2010					
1/1	Balance	✔			3 9 2 1 0
11/30	Balance	✔			2 4 9 9 3 0

ACCOUNT: Petty Cash   105

DATE	EXPLANATION	REF.	DEBIT	CREDIT	BALANCE
2010					
1/1	Balance	✔			1 5 0

ACCOUNT: Accounts Receivable   112

DATE	EXPLANATION	REF.	DEBIT	CREDIT	BALANCE
2010					
1/1	Balance	✔			2 5 3 6 4 3
11/30	Balance	✔			3 1 7 4 2 0
12/3		J 9		3 7 0 0	3 1 3 7 2 0
12/15		J 9		4 6 8 0	3 0 9 0 4 0
12/17		J 9		4 5 2 0 0	2 6 3 8 4 0

GENERAL LEDGER ACCOUNTS

ACCOUNT: Allowance for Doubtful Accounts 113

DATE	EXPLANATION	REF.		DEBIT	CREDIT	BALANCE
2010						
1/1	Balance	✔				1 3 5 2 0
11/30	Balance	✔				4 5 8 0
12/3		J	9	3 7 0 0		8 8 0

ACCOUNT: Notes Receivable 115

DATE	EXPLANATION	REF.		DEBIT	CREDIT	BALANCE
2010						
1/1	Balance	✔				4 0 0 0 0
11/30	Balance–Platteville Plumbers	✔				4 5 0 0 0
12/17	Bilder Construction	J	9	4 5 2 0 0		9 0 2 0 0

ACCOUNT: Interest Receivable 118

DATE	EXPLANATION	REF.		DEBIT	CREDIT	BALANCE
2010						
1/1	Balance	✔				5 8 0
11/30	Balance	✔				- 0 -

ACCOUNT: Merchandise Inventory 120

DATE	EXPLANATION	REF.		DEBIT	CREDIT	BALANCE
2010						
1/1	Balance	✔				450960
11/30	Balance	✔				531960
12/13		CR	12		9834	522126
12/15		J	9	3550		525676
12/15		J	9		3550	522126
12/20		CD	18	1021		523147
12/23		J	9	2300		525447

ACCOUNT: Office Supplies 125

DATE	EXPLANATION	REF.		DEBIT	CREDIT	BALANCE
2010						
1/1	Balance	✔				470
11/30	Balance	✔				2320
12/21		CD	18	1360		3680

ACCOUNT: Prepaid Insurance 130

DATE	EXPLANATION	REF.		DEBIT	CREDIT	BALANCE
2010						
1/1	Balance	✔				3970
11/30	Balance	✔				11020

ACCOUNT: Prepaid Rent   131

DATE	EXPLANATION	REF.	DEBIT	CREDIT	BALANCE
2010					
1/1	Balance	✔			3630
11/30	Balance	✔			25410

ACCOUNT: Other Assets   135

DATE	EXPLANATION	REF.		DEBIT	CREDIT	BALANCE
2010						
1/1	Balance	✔				130000
7/1		CD	15	15000		145000

ACCOUNT: Land   140

DATE	EXPLANATION	REF.	DEBIT	CREDIT	BALANCE
2010					
1/1	Balance	✔			43000

ACCOUNT: Buildings   145

DATE	EXPLANATION	REF.	DEBIT	CREDIT	BALANCE
2010					
1/1	Balance	✔			306000

ACCOUNT: Accum. Depr.–Buildings 146

DATE	EXPLANATION	REF.	DEBIT	CREDIT	BALANCE
2010					
1/1	Balance	✔			7 3 0 4 0

ACCOUNT: Office Equipment 151

DATE	EXPLANATION	REF.	DEBIT	CREDIT	BALANCE
2010					
1/1	Balance	✔			3 2 8 0 0
12/23		CD 18	6 1 0 0		3 8 9 0 0

ACCOUNT: Accum. Depr.–Off. Equip. 152

DATE	EXPLANATION	REF.	DEBIT	CREDIT	BALANCE
2010					
1/1	Balance	✔			1 3 2 0 0

ACCOUNT: Delivery Trucks 163

DATE	EXPLANATION	REF.	DEBIT	CREDIT	BALANCE
2010					
1/1	Balance	✔			7 8 4 0 0

ACCOUNT: Accum. Depr.–Delivery Trucks 164

DATE	EXPLANATION	REF.		DEBIT	CREDIT	BALANCE
2010						
1/1	Balance	✔				3 9 5 4 0

ACCOUNT: Notes Payable 200

DATE	EXPLANATION	REF.		DEBIT	CREDIT	BALANCE
2010						
1/1	Balance–renewed 12/31/09	✔				1 5 0 0 0

ACCOUNT: Accounts Payable 201

DATE	EXPLANATION	REF.		DEBIT	CREDIT	BALANCE
2010						
1/1	Balance	✔				8 6 3 5 2
11/30	Balance	✔				1 2 6 8 5 0
12/15		J	9	3 5 5 0		1 2 3 3 0 0
12/22		CD	18		5 5 0 0	1 2 8 8 0 0
12/23		J	9		2 3 0 0	1 3 1 1 0 0

ACCOUNT: Wages Payable 211

DATE	EXPLANATION	REF.	DEBIT	CREDIT	BALANCE
2010					
1/1	Balance	✔			1906
⌇					⌇
11/30	Balance	✔			-0-

ACCOUNT: FICA Taxes Payable 214

DATE	EXPLANATION	REF.		DEBIT	CREDIT	BALANCE
2010						
1/1	Balance	✔				781
⌇						⌇
11/30	Balance	✔				1787
12/7		CD	18		350	2137
12/7		J	9		350	2487
12/16		CD	18	1787		700
12/21		J	9		415	1115
12/21		CD	18		415	1530

ACCOUNT: Federal Income Taxes Payable 215

DATE	EXPLANATION	REF.	DEBIT	CREDIT	BALANCE
2010					
1/1	Balance	✔			15789
⌇					⌇
11/30	Balance	✔			-0-

ACCOUNT: Federal Income Tax Withhldg Payable   216

DATE	EXPLANATION	REF.		DEBIT	CREDIT	BALANCE
2010						
1/1	Balance	✔				5148
11/30	Balance	✔				9573
12/7		CD	18		900	10473
12/16		CD	18	9573		900
12/21		CD	18		1067	1967

ACCOUNT: State Income Tax Withhldg Payable   218

DATE	EXPLANATION	REF.		DEBIT	CREDIT	BALANCE
2010						
1/1	Balance	✔				1595
11/30	Balance	✔				2486
12/7		CD	18		190	2676
12/21		CD	18		225	2901

ACCOUNT: Federal Unemployment Taxes Payable   224

DATE	EXPLANATION	REF.		DEBIT	CREDIT	BALANCE
2010						
1/1	Balance	✔				216
11/30	Balance	✔				400

GENERAL LEDGER ACCOUNTS

ACCOUNT: State Unemployment Taxes Payable   226

DATE	EXPLANATION	REF.	DEBIT	CREDIT	BALANCE
2010					
1/1	Balance	✔			1323
11/30	Balance	✔			2600

ACCOUNT: Interest Payable   230

DATE	EXPLANATION	REF.	DEBIT	CREDIT	BALANCE
2010					
1/1	Balance	✔			15165
11/30	Balance	✔			-0-

ACCOUNT: Dividends Payable   250

DATE	EXPLANATION	REF.	DEBIT	CREDIT	BALANCE
2010					
1/1	Balance	✔			23100
11/30	Balance	✔			-0-

ACCOUNT: Notes Payable (LT Liability)   268

DATE	EXPLANATION	REF.	DEBIT	CREDIT	BALANCE
2010					
1/1	Balance	✔			43000
7/1	Increased Mortgage	CR 10		70000	113000

ACCOUNT: Bonds Payable   270

DATE	EXPLANATION	REF.	DEBIT	CREDIT	BALANCE
2010					
1/1	Balance (issued Mar. 1, 2004)	✔			275000

ACCOUNT: Discount on Bonds Payable   273

DATE	EXPLANATION	REF.	DEBIT	CREDIT	BALANCE
2010					
1/1	Balance	✔			4400

ACCOUNT: Common Stock–$30 Stated Value   311

DATE	EXPLANATION	REF.	DEBIT	CREDIT	BALANCE
2010					
1/1	Balance (6,300 shares)	✔			189000

ACCOUNT: P-I-C in Excess of Stated Value   317

DATE	EXPLANATION	REF.	DEBIT	CREDIT	BALANCE
2010					
1/1	Balance	✔			256400

GENERAL LEDGER ACCOUNTS

ACCOUNT: Retained Earnings   320

DATE	EXPLANATION	REF.	DEBIT	CREDIT	BALANCE
2010					
1/1	Balance	✔			362748

ACCOUNT: Treasury Stock-Common   330

DATE	EXPLANATION	REF.	DEBIT	CREDIT	BALANCE
2010					
1/1	Balance (700 shares)	✔			44610

ACCOUNT: Dividends Declared   333

DATE	EXPLANATION	REF.	DEBIT	CREDIT	BALANCE
2010					

ACCOUNT: Income Summary   350

DATE	EXPLANATION	REF.	DEBIT	CREDIT	BALANCE
2010					

ACCOUNT: Sales   401

DATE	EXPLANATION	REF.	DEBIT	CREDIT	BALANCE
2010					
11/30	Balance	✔			5 2 3 4 9 4 0

ACCOUNT: Sales Returns and Allowances   412

DATE	EXPLANATION	REF.	DEBIT	CREDIT	BALANCE
2010					
11/30	Balance	✔			9 3 8 0
12/15		J 9	4 6 8 0		1 4 0 6 0

ACCOUNT: Sales Discounts   414

DATE	EXPLANATION	REF.	DEBIT	CREDIT	BALANCE
2010					
11/30	Balance	✔			7 3 0 4 4

GENERAL LEDGER ACCOUNTS

ACCOUNT: Cost of Goods Sold 505

DATE	EXPLANATION	REF.		DEBIT	CREDIT	BALANCE
2010						
11/30	Balance	✔				3 648 7 2 2
12/13		CR	12	9834		3 658 5 5 6
12/15		J	9		3550	3 655 0 0 6

ACCOUNT: Advertising Expenses 610

DATE	EXPLANATION	REF.		DEBIT	CREDIT	BALANCE
2010						
11/30	Balance	✔				6578
12/9		CD	18	600		7178

ACCOUNT: Bad Debt Expense 612

DATE	EXPLANATION	REF.		DEBIT	CREDIT	BALANCE
2010						

ACCOUNT: Depreciation Expense–Trucks 617

DATE	EXPLANATION	REF.		DEBIT	CREDIT	BALANCE
2010						

GENERAL LEDGER ACCOUNTS

ACCOUNT: Sales Salaries Expense 627

DATE	EXPLANATION	REF.	DEBIT	CREDIT	BALANCE
2010					
11/30	Balance	✔			132990

ACCOUNT: Wage Expense 643

DATE	EXPLANATION	REF.	DEBIT	CREDIT	BALANCE
2010					
11/30	Balance	✔			110616
12/7		CD 18	4860		115476
12/21		CD 18	5770		121246

ACCOUNT: Freight-out 644

DATE	EXPLANATION	REF.	DEBIT	CREDIT	BALANCE
2010					
11/30	Balance	✔			17732
12/6		CD 18	810		18542

ACCOUNT: Miscellaneous Selling Expense 649

DATE	EXPLANATION	REF.	DEBIT	CREDIT	BALANCE
2010					

ACCOUNT: Depreciation Expense–Buildings   713

DATE	EXPLANATION	REF.	DEBIT	CREDIT	BALANCE
2010					

ACCOUNT: Depreciation Expense–Off. Equip.   715

DATE	EXPLANATION	REF.	DEBIT	CREDIT	BALANCE
2010					

ACCOUNT: Insurance Expense   722

DATE	EXPLANATION	REF.	DEBIT	CREDIT	BALANCE
2010					

GENERAL LEDGER ACCOUNTS

ACCOUNT: Office Salaries Expense   727

DATE	EXPLANATION	REF.	DEBIT	CREDIT	BALANCE
2010					
11/30	Balance	✔			6 8 9 5 1 6

ACCOUNT: Office Supplies Expense   728

DATE	EXPLANATION	REF.	DEBIT	CREDIT	BALANCE
2010					
11/30	Balance	✔			1 5 4 0

ACCOUNT: Rent Expenses   729

DATE	EXPLANATION	REF.	DEBIT	CREDIT	BALANCE
2010					

ACCOUNT: Payroll Taxes Expense   730

DATE	EXPLANATION	REF.	DEBIT	CREDIT	BALANCE
2010					
11/30	Balance	✔			8 2 9 1 6
12/7		J 9	3 5 0		8 3 2 6 6
12/21		J 9	4 1 5		8 3 6 8 1

GENERAL LEDGER ACCOUNTS

ACCOUNT: Utilities Expense   732

DATE	EXPLANATION	REF.	DEBIT	CREDIT	BALANCE
2010					
11/30	Balance	✔			16270
12/15		CD 18	399		16669

ACCOUNT: Interest Revenue   820

DATE	EXPLANATION	REF.	DEBIT	CREDIT	BALANCE
2010					
11/30	Balance	✔			3150

ACCOUNT: Gain on Plant Assets   826

DATE	EXPLANATION	REF.	DEBIT	CREDIT	BALANCE
2010					

ACCOUNT: Interest Expense   905

DATE	EXPLANATION	REF.	DEBIT	CREDIT	BALANCE
2010					
11/30	Balance	✔			2 4 5 7 0

ACCOUNT: Loss on Plant Assets   921

DATE	EXPLANATION	REF.	DEBIT	CREDIT	BALANCE
2010					

ACCOUNT: Income Tax Expense   999

DATE	EXPLANATION	REF.	DEBIT	CREDIT	BALANCE
2010					
11/30	Balance	✔			7 2 0 0 0

SUBSIDIARY LEDGERS

ACCOUNT: Boecker Builders   117

DATE	EXPLANATION	REF.	DEBIT	CREDIT	BALANCE
2010					
11/30	Balance	✔			6 2 9 2 0
12/9	1050 &	1071		2 9 0 0 0	3 3 9 2 0
12/13		1071		3 3 9 2 0	- 0 -
12/14		1207	2 1 7 3 0		2 1 7 3 0

ACCOUNT: The Potts Company   122

DATE	EXPLANATION	REF.	DEBIT	CREDIT	BALANCE
2010					
11/30	Balance	✔			5 0 3 0 0
12/6		1128		5 0 3 0 0	- 0 -
12/13		1206	3 1 4 5 0		3 1 4 5 0
12/15		1206		4 6 8 0	2 6 7 7 0

ACCOUNT: Swanson Brothers Construction   133

DATE	EXPLANATION	REF.	DEBIT	CREDIT	BALANCE
2010					
11/30	Balance	✔			2 4 0 5 0
12/1		1120		2 4 0 5 0	- 0 -

ACCOUNT: A & B Hardware   143

DATE	EXPLANATION	REF.	DEBIT	CREDIT	BALANCE
2010					
12/17		1208	7 9 2 0		7 9 2 0

ACCOUNT: Trudy's Plumbing   155

DATE	EXPLANATION	REF.	DEBIT	CREDIT	BALANCE
2010					
11/30	Balance	✔			15100
12/8		1204	26300		41400
12/10		1106		15100	26300
12/10		1205	24850		51150
12/14		1204		26300	24850
12/20		1205		24850	-0-

ACCOUNT: Coconino Contractors, Inc   160

DATE	EXPLANATION	REF.	DEBIT	CREDIT	BALANCE
2010					
11/30	Balance	✔			27800
12/6		1203	10300		38100
12/8		1091		27800	10300
12/20		1209	42780		53080

ACCOUNT: Rankin Plumbing Corp.   166

DATE	EXPLANATION	REF.	DEBIT	CREDIT	BALANCE
2010					
11/30	Balance	✔			74350
12/7		1129		74350	-0-

ACCOUNT: Beverly's Building Products   175

DATE	EXPLANATION	REF.	DEBIT	CREDIT	BALANCE
2010					
11/30	Balance	✔			14000
12/1		1201	13150		27150

ACCOUNTS RECEIVABLE SUBSIDIARY LEDGER

ACCOUNT: Bilder Construction Company   180

DATE	EXPLANATION	REF.	DEBIT	CREDIT	BALANCE
2010					
11/30	Balance	✔			45200
12/3		1202	44900		90100
12/17		1120		45200	44900

ACCOUNT: Iwanaga Plumbing and Heating   190

DATE	EXPLANATION	REF.	DEBIT	CREDIT	BALANCE
2010					
11/30	Balance	✔			3700
12/3	Write-Off	780		3700	-0-

ACCOUNT:

DATE	EXPLANATION	REF.	DEBIT	CREDIT	BALANCE
2010					

ACCOUNT:

DATE	EXPLANATION	REF.	DEBIT	CREDIT	BALANCE
2010					

ACCOUNT: Phoenix Plastics   14

DATE	EXPLANATION	REF.	DEBIT	CREDIT	BALANCE
2010					
11/30	Balance	✔			17450
12/7		313	10700		6750
12/8	1/10, n/30	316		52700	59450
12/9		299	6750		52700
12/16		316	52700		-0-
12/22	1/10, n/30	319		48330	48330

ACCOUNT: Business Basics, Inc.   16

DATE	EXPLANATION	REF.	DEBIT	CREDIT	BALANCE
2010					
12/22	n/30	318		5500	5500

ACCOUNT: Edward's Plumbing Supplies, Inc.   18

DATE	EXPLANATION	REF.	DEBIT	CREDIT	BALANCE
2010					
11/30	Balance	✔			20050
12/2	n/60	315		24320	44370
12/15		315	3550		40820

ACCOUNT: DeKalb Transport   20

DATE	EXPLANATION	REF.	DEBIT	CREDIT	BALANCE
2010					
12/23	n/30	J 9		2300	2300

ACCOUNT: Oxenford Copperworks   35

DATE	EXPLANATION	REF.	DEBIT	CREDIT	BALANCE
2010					
11/30	Balance	✔			26400
12/2		280	26400		-0-

ACCOUNT: Smith Pipe Company   39

DATE	EXPLANATION	REF.	DEBIT	CREDIT	BALANCE
2010					
11/30	Balance	✔			38100
12/10		314	38100		-0-
12/17	1/15, n/60	317		43800	43800

ACCOUNT: Ron & Rod's Plumbing Products   44

DATE	EXPLANATION	REF.	DEBIT	CREDIT	BALANCE
2010					
11/30	Balance	✔			14850

ACCOUNT: Khatan Steel Corp.   57

DATE	EXPLANATION	REF.	DEBIT	CREDIT	BALANCE
2010					
11/30	Balance	✔			10000
12/7		312	10000		-0-

ACCOUNTS PAYABLE SUBSIDIARY LEDGER

ACCOUNT: Northern Electric Co.

DATE	EXPLANATION	REF.	DEBIT	CREDIT	BALANCE
2010					

ACCOUNT: City of Rockford

DATE	EXPLANATION	REF.	DEBIT	CREDIT	BALANCE
2010					

TEN-COLUMN WORKSHEET

ACCOUNT TITLES	TRIAL BALANCE		ADJUSTMENTS	
	DR.	CR.	DR.	CR.
Cash				
Petty Cash				
Accounts Receivable				
Allowance for Doubtful Accounts				
Notes Receivable				
Interest Receivable				
Merchandise Inventory				
Office Supplies				
Prepaid Insurance				
Prepaid Rent				
Other Assets				
Land				
Buildings				
Accum. Depr. - Buildings				
Office Equipment				
Accum. Depr. - Off. Equip.				
Delivery Trucks				
Accum. Depr. - Delivery Trucks				
Notes Payable				
Accounts Payable				
Wages Payable				
Salaries Payable				
FICA Taxes Payable				
Federal Income Taxes Payable				
Federal Withhldg Tax Payable				
State Withhldg Tax Payable				
Federal Unemployment Taxes Pay.				
State Unemployment Taxes Pay.				
Interest Payable				
Dividends Payable				
Notes Payable (LT Liability)				
Bonds Payable				
Discount on Bonds Payable				
Common Stock				
P-I-C in Excess of Stated Value				
Retained Earnings				
Treasury Stock - Common				
Dividends Declared				
Income Summary				
Sales				
Sales Returns and Allowances				
Sales Discounts				
Subtotals				

ADJUSTED TRIAL BALANCE		INCOME STATEMENT		BALANCE SHEET	
DR.	CR.	DR.	CR.	DR.	CR.

ACCOUNT TITLES	TRIAL BALANCE		ADJUSTMENTS	
	DR.	CR.	DR.	CR.
Cost of Goods Sold				
Advertising Expenses				
Bad Debt Expense				
Depreciation Expense–Trucks				
Sales Salaries Expense				
Wage Expense				
Freight-Out				
Miscellaneous Selling Expense				
Depreciation Expense–Buildings				
Depreciation Expense–Off. Equip.				
Insurance Expense				
Office Salaries Expense				
Office Supplies Expense				
Rent Expenses				
Payroll Taxes Expense				
Utilities Expense				
Interest Revenue				
Gain on Plant Assets				
Interest Expense				
Loss on Plant Assets				
Income Tax Expense				
Totals				
Income Tax Expense				
Federal Income Taxes Payable				
Net Income				
Totals				

ADJUSTED TRIAL BALANCE		INCOME STATEMENT		BALANCE SHEET	
DR.	CR.	DR.	CR.	DR.	CR.

SCHEDULES AND FINANCIAL STATEMENTS

SCHEDULE OF ACCOUNTS RECEIVABLE
SCHEDULE OF ACCOUNTS PAYABLE
INCOME STATEMENT
STATEMENT OF RETAINED EARNINGS
BALANCE SHEET
STATEMENT OF CASH FLOWS
POST-CLOSING TRIAL BALANCE

SCHEDULE OF ACCOUNTS RECEIVABLE
SCHEDULE OF ACCOUNTS PAYABLE

SCHEDULE OF ACCOUNTS RECEIVABLE

117	Boecker Builders	4 2 0 4 0		
122	The Potts Company	2 6 7 7 0		
133	Swanson Brothers Construction	2 4 6 5 0		
143	A+B Hardware	7 9 2 0		
155	Trudy's Plumbing	5 5 7 7 0		
160	Coconino Contractors, Inc.	5 3 0 8 0		
166	Rankin Plumbing Corp.	—		
175	Beverly's Building Products	1 3 1 5 0		
180	Bilder Construction Company	4 4 9 0 0		
190	Iwanaga Plumbing and Heating	—		
	Total Accounts Receivable			2 6 8 2 8 0

SCHEDULE OF ACCOUNTS PAYABLE

14	Phoenix Plastics	4 8 3 3 0		
16	Business Basics, Inc.	5 5 0 0		
18	Edward's Plumbing Supplies, Inc.	4 0 8 2 0		
20	Dekalb Transport	2 3 0 0		
35	Oxenford Copperworks	5 5 9 4 0		
39	Smith Pipe Company	—		
44	Ron + Rod's Plumbing Products	1 4 8 5 0		
57	Khatan Steel Corp.	—		
	Northern Electric Co.	5 3 0		
	City of Rockford	2 7 9		
	Total Accounts Payable			1 6 8 5 4 9

Rockford Corporation
Income Statement
For the Year Ended December 31, 2010

	Col 1	Col 2	Col 3	Col 4
Sales Revenue				5619052
Less: Sales Discounts			14060	
Sales Returns and Allowances			77041	91101
Net Sales Revenue				5527951
Cost of Goods Sold				3952462
Gross Profit on Sales				1575489
Operating Expenses				
Selling Expenses				
Advertising Expense	7678			
Depreciation Expense – Trucks	21160			
Sales Salaries Expense	148990			
Wage Expense	126846			
Freight-Out	19541			
Miscellaneous Selling Expense	587	324802		
Administrative Expenses				
Depreciation Expense – Buildings	4400			
Depreciation Expense – Off. Equip.	4603			
Insurance Expense	1763			
Office Salaries Expense	712416			
Office Supplies Expense	4458			
Rent Expense	7260			
Payroll Tax Expense	84056			
Utilities Expense	17478			
Bad Debt Expenses	110559	946993		1271795
Income from Operations				303694
Other Revenues and Gains				
Interest Revenue				3150
				306844
Other Expenses and Losses				
Interest Expense			56220	
Loss on Plant Assets			400	56620
Income before income Tax				250224
Income Tax				94669
Net Income				155555
Earnings per common share				27 78

Rockford Corporation
Statement of Retained Earnings
For the Year Ended December 31, 2010

Retained Earning Beginning Balance 1/1/10		362748
Add: Net Income		155555
Retained Earnings		518303
Less: Dividends		14310
Retained Earnings Ending Balance 12/31/10		503993

Current Assets			
Cash		273548	
Accounts Receivable	268280		
Less: Allowance for Doubtful Accounts	111439	156841	
Notes Receivable		104200	
Merchandise Inventory		451421	
Office Supplies		830	
Prepaid Insurance		8670	
Prepaid Rent		18150	
Other Assets		160000	
Total Current Assets			1173660
Property, Plant, and Equipment			
Land		99650	
Buildings	306000		
Less: Accumulated Depreciation	77440	228560	
Office Equipment	38900		
Less: Accumulated Depreciation	17803	21097	
Delivery Trucks	70500		
Less: Accumulated Depreciation	55700	14800	
Total Property, Plant, and Equipment			364107
Total Assets			1537767

Current Liabilities			
Notes Payable		15000	
Accounts Payable		168549	
Wages Payable		3971	
FICA Taxes Payable		4400	
Federal Income Taxes Payable		22669	
Federal Income Tax Withhldg Payable		16199	
State Income Tax Withhldg Payable		4636	
Federal Unemployment Tax Payable		400	
State Unemployment Tax Payable		2600	
Interest Payable		30770	
Dividends Payable		14310	
Total Current Assets			277504
Long Term Liabilities			
Notes Payable		113000	
Bonds Payable	275000		
Less: Discount on Bonds Payable	3520	271480	
Total Long Term Liabilities			384480
Total Liabilities			661984
Stockholder's Equity			
Common Stock		207000	
P-I-C in Excess Stated Value		292400	499400
Retained Earnings			503993
Less: Treasury Stock			(127410)
Total Stockholders Equity			875783
Total Liabilities and Stockholders Equity			1537767

Cash Flows from Operating Activities			
Net Income			155555
Adjustments to reconcile net income to net cash			
Depreciation Expense		30163	
Loss on Sale of Equipment		400	
Increase in Accounts Receivable		(14637)	
Increase in Inventories		(461)	
Increase in Prepaid Expenses		(19220)	
Increase in Accounts Payable		82197	
Increase in Accrued Expenses Payable		54966	133408
Net Cash provided by Operating Activities			288963
Cash Flows from Investing Activities			
Sale of Delivery Trucks		7900	
Purchase of Land		(56650)	
Purchase of Equipment		(6100)	
Net Cash used by Investing Activities			(54850)
Net Increase In Cash			234113
Cash at beginning period			39210
Cash at end of period			273323

Rockford Corporation
Post-Closing Trial Balance
December 31, 2010

Account	Debit	Credit
Cash	273323	
Petty Cash	225	
Accounts Receivable	268280	
Allowance for Doubtful Accounts		11439
Notes Receivable	104200	
Merchandise Inventory	451421	
Office Supplies	830	
Prepaid Insurance	8670	
Prepaid Rent	18150	
Other Assets	160000	
Land	99650	
Buildings	306000	
Accum. Depr. – Buildings		77440
Office Equipment	38900	
Accum. Depr. – Off. Equip.		17803
Delivery Trucks	70500	
Accum. Depr. – Delivery Trucks		55700
Notes Payable		15000
Accounts Payable		168549
Wages Payable		3971
FICA Taxes Payable		4400
Federal Income Taxes Payable		22669
Federal Income Tax Withhldg Payable		10199
State Income Tax Withhldg Payable		4636
Federal Unemployment Taxes Payable		400
State Unemployment Taxes Payable		2600
Interest Payable		30770
Dividends Payable		14310
Notes Payable (LT Liabilities)		113000
Bonds Payable		275000
Discount on Bonds Payable	3520	
Common Stock		207000
P-I-C in Excess of Stated Value		292400
Retained Earnings		503913
Treasury Stock	127610	
	1931279	1931279